IRELAND ON THREE
MILLION POUNDS A DAY

Declan Lynch

N E W
ISLAND
BOOKS

Dublin

Ireland on Three Million Pounds a Day
is first published in 1995 by
New Island Books
2, Brookside,
Dundrum Road,
Dublin 14,
Ireland

ISBN 1 874597 29 4

New Island Books receives financial assistance from
The Arts Council (An Chomhairle Ealaíon),
Dublin, Ireland.

Cover illustration by Jon Berkeley
Typeset by Graphic Resources
Printed in Ireland by Colour Books Ltd.

Contents

Let us name the guilty men and women. Dermot Bolger, poet, playwright, novelist and publisher is the Mr Big of this project, the boss man directing operations with an unseen hand. Something about his initial phone-call suggested to me that if I failed to comply with his wishes, I would sleep with the fishes.

Anthony Glavin of New Island Books was his enforcer, a charming guy who speaks softly and carries a big stick. You wouldn't mess with Mr Tony Glavin. You leave a manuscript on Tony's doorstep and run all the way home.

Anne Harris, my sainted editor at the *Sunday Independent*, is also complicit in this document, having run sections of it in the paper on a weekly basis despite the reasonable objections of those citizens who convey their anger in floods of green biro.

If we go to the root of it all, then Niall Stokes, editor of *Hot Press*, is the boss of bosses, the *capo di tutti capo*. Niall gave me "the start". And he has given me the odd start ever since.

Don't shoot me, I'm only the piano-player.

Declan Lynch
October 1995

"If you don't live in a democracy, you risk your life for saying things. In a democracy, you say things and they laugh at you."

— *Tom Mathews, cartoonist*

EMINENT ATHLONIANS

ATHLONE vs AC MILAN

*Athlone, Ireland (UPI): Athlone Town, a collection of Sunday afternoon footballers who earn £12 a week, held the mighty AC Milan to a 0-0 draw today in the second round of the UEFA Cup in Athlone. The Irishmen came close to defeating the Italian club, whose players are worth about $5 million in transfer fees. But winger John Minnock missed a thirty-minute penalty. Athlone was awarded the kick when Scala brought down Daly, but Minnock's weak shot was stopped by Albertosi, who also had to pull off a series of first-half saves to keep the Irish men off the score-board. A crowd of 12,000, which is Athlone's population, crammed into St Mel's Park ground to watch the match which local historians claimed was the biggest thing to happen since the Earl of Lucan burned down the town's bridge in the seventeeth-century. The Italians brought their own chef, wine and food to boost their morale. They made almost no effort to attack, and only came into the game when Athlone appeared to run out of steam after seventy minutes. "We should have won," said Athlone manager Amby Fogarty, "but I am happy with a draw." AC Milan manager Nereo Rocco was tight-lipped after the game. "I said I would be happy with a draw. I still am," he snapped. (**From the New York Herald Tribune**).*

On a bright crisp Autumn day in 1975, the attention of the Universe was focussed on St Mel's Park, Athlone, and a UEFA Cup clash between The Town and AC Milan. We were much misunderstood in Athlone since the last time our exploits had hit the world headlines. A certain bitterness had set in after our deepest misfortunes had generated such widespread hilarity. Goalkeeper Mick O'Brien's crossbar-breaking episode in an FAI Cup semi-final against Finn Harps at Oriel Park travelled far and wide. He was not to know that some crossbars are made of inferior material to the durable metal structures which were *de rigueur* at St Mel's, and he suffered cruelly for his athleticism. We all did.

And now as the world's media came along once more to laugh their heads off at us, it was time to settle a grudge or two.

Oh, they laughed all right at the idea of million-dollar Italian superstars having to sluice their expensive torsos beneath "showers" which squirted an unpredictable brackish fluid, and which had a choice of two temperatures — freezing cold or boiling hot. To which we said: "Fuck those people. If they want a shower, they can queue up like anyone else in front of the hose." They laughed too at the excellent performance of the pipe band who adorned the preliminaries with a rousing selection of traditional airs, led by a goat. I laughed a bit myself, to tell you the truth. We all did. All except the goat. They laughed indeed at what they saw as the basically preposterous nature of the whole scenario, as the credentials and occupations of the Athlone players became more exotically miserable with every preview.

We knew different. We knew that our boys had dumped the crack Norwegian outfit Valerengen out of the first round on a 4-2 aggregate, blossoming in the white heat of St Mel's, and consolidating in the black ice of the frozen North. Supremo Amby Fogarty had assembled a powerful squad built around the mature talents of the wily schemer Dougie Wood, featuring some take-no-prisoners Derrymen in defence, the breathtaking industry of play-maker John Minnock, the elusive wing artistry of Terry Daly, and the devastating twin spearhead of Paul Martin and Eugene "Pooch" Davis. Not to mention the legendary Mick O'Brien, secure between reinforced platinum goalposts.

Those Italian aristos put up a good front, all right, preening extravagantly in the pre-match kickabout, flaunting their beautifully-honed physiques, all rippling bronze thighs and balletic elegance, as they strove to freak out the cadaverous natives with their Class. Gianni Rivera, Latin idol, didn't tog out, but strolled about in the nicest overcoat anyone had ever seen. And there was captain Romeo Benetti, he whose rich skills were matched only by his boundless cynicism in the tackle. And Albertosi, the goalkeeper, whom we last saw picking it out of the cobwebs four times against Brazil in the Azteca Stadium, in the final of Mexico '70.

We were fairly impressed, to be sure, but we also knew by a certain glide in their stride that The Town had their dander cranked up to maximum overload. And the saps were rising as our no-nonsense warriors gave as good as they got in the opening passages, and gave it even when they weren't getting it, as such. Around the half-hour mark, the Pizza Men suddenly discovered the rancid taste of workhouse gruel. An explosive burst into the area by Terry Daly left the cynical full-back with no alternative but to scythe him down like a dog. Penalty !!!

The next couple of minutes are branded forever on my memory in eerie, dream-like, slow motion. Amid scenes of total dementia, John Minnock, whose educated left foot could have given post-graduate tutorials at the Sorbonne, placed the ball on the spot. The doomed Albertosi faced up to his grim destiny, his mind probably haunted by flashbacks of what Pele, Gerson, Jairzinho, and Carlos Alberto had done to him in the cauldron of the Azteca.

Minnock essayed a short run-up and stroked the leather to Albertosi's right. The ball sort of...staggered...into his grateful clutches, and pandemonium switched instantly to the tortured silence of 12,000 Midlanders finding themselves in the very Vortex of Hades.

Both teams were so stunned by the enormity of what had happened that they were unable thereafter to lift the wicked spell, and fought out a, shall we say, "manly" encounter without breaking the deadlock. The final score read a stupendous 0-0 victory for Athlone Town. The second leg in the San Siro Stadium saw another bloody magnificent display by The Town, whom AC Milan may have mistaken for city rivals Internazionale, who model their kit on Athlone's black-and-blue stripes.

We all watched the game on the radio, agog with the prospect of further glory, as Philip Greene, with an hour gone and still no surrender by Town, began speculating as to who would do the honours in a penalty shoot-out, in the light of recent painful events.

Then Milan scored three goals.

But I digress. For the Italians, it was the final futile flourish of desperate men. Our war was over and we had won, goddammit.

JOHN MC CORMACK — THE CHINESE CONNECTION

It was not the first time that Milan had been trounced by Athlone. La Scala may be the world's most prestigious Opera House (not to mention the name of the defender who chopped down Terry Daly) but for a long time, a Shannon-sider by the name of John McCormack sang the cream of Italian manhood off the stage.

In recent times, it came to light that McCormack's birthplace is now a Chinese take-away. Row Inn Row, to be precise. The fact that it is situated in one of the oldest areas of the town, The Bawn, led to one wag calling the place the Old Walled City. The mejia had a lot of sport with it, and someone floated a rumour that it was all a Masonic conspiracy.

I spurn such bleatings as I would spurn a Progressive Democrat in heat. In any case, there is an excellent bust on the Shannon bank of John McCormack — or at least a John McCormack. Looks aren't everything.

There was also a lot of whingeing about the plaque outside the Chinese take-away, which contains the legend *Worlds Famous Tenor*, with no apostrophe in *Worlds*. There was also the suggestion that *Worlds* should not be pluralised. To counter this, I merely have to point to the long-standing belief among Athlone people like myself, that this little planet of ours may not be the only World in the Universe, hence the pluralisation on the plaque, and suggest that if there are other Worlds out there, it is incredibly unlikely that any of their inhabitants can sing *Macushla* with as much *cojones* as our John.

The idea of a Masonic conspiracy to downgrade the reputation of the man who was the Pavarotti of his day, with less whale-fat, may be rooted in the fact that McCormack, when he gave forth such monster hits as *Panis Angelicus* at the Eucharistic Congress, was allying himself too closely with the Papacy, which duly awarded him with the rather enigmatic nickname,

"Count". (He shared it with a black man by the name of Basie, who never had half his talent).

But I happen to know that McCormack also hung out with some of Chicago's most spectacular gangsters at a time when Chicago gangsterdom was at its spectacular zenith. He was also on more than nodding terms with one Eamonn de Valera, a fellow artist who is best remembered for writing some additional material in a notorious short novel by John Charles McQuaid, called *Bunreacht Na hEireann*.

You see, everyone loved John McCormack, regardless of creed or colour or sexual orientation or criminal record. To criticise the idea of his birthplace being a Chinese take-away, ignores the fact that the primary function of Irish artists is to persuade foreign visitors to disport themselves in establishments which bear the artist's name many years after they have turned up their toes. Even now, I sense that someone is devising the Samuel Beckett Diner in Temple Bar, where you eat your dinner out of dustbins. It could happen, because when Beckett died, there was a rash of newspaper articles by people who claimed to have had convivial bottles of stout with the great man, during which he would make telling remarks like "Glory be, is that the time already? I don't want to be late for the Wham! concert." Far from being the recluse of legend, you got the impression that he must have been one of the most sociable men in Paris. "Eat At Sam's...You Can't Go On, But You'll Go On!" Being discreet, the Athlone Chinese reject such ostentation.

Martin Dully, the former Bord Failte chief, has an inkling of the damage that such Cultural Tourism can wreak. Like myself and John McCormack, he was a pupil of Marist College, Athlone, though only one of us became a world-famous tenor. Martin was clearly singing for Ireland though, when he told Gay Byrne that, sitting on the bridge below the town, as a boy during the 1940s, watching the flow of traffic to the West, he sometimes felt that he was at the crossroads of the World. And any man who can view Athlone during the 40s as the crossroads of the World was the right man to be running Bord Failte.

Other major Athlone artists include John Broderick, the first man from the town to write a novel in some 700 years. While he attracted a fair amount of dog's abuse for his pioneering efforts — he alleged that Midlanders engaged in sexual practices, and that some of them did it with priests — little of it emanated from Athlone people, who just regretted that he couldn't sing very well.

To a degree, the massive shadow of McCormack has haunted the creative spirit of Midlanders in the way that Joyce has intimidated Dublin writers. And Joyce, of course, with a fine tenor voice himself, really wanted to be McCormack, whereas McCormack wanted to be Pope Pius, Legs Diamond, and God, eventually settling for the latter.

He certainly gave the lie to all those taunts about the Midland timbre being "flat". Those fabulous lungs of his never uttered a single flat note. Something to do with a few spare ribs, I'd guess.

As for John Broderick, I wrote his obituary. I wrote it when he was still alive, in fact. It is standard practice for newspapers to run a "morgue" full of ready-to-use obituaries, because people tend not to inform the papers in advance that they are planning to pop their clogs. It's a bit like one of those TV cookery programmes — here's one that we prepared before the show. A journalist of my acquaintance who presided over his paper's morgue, thought that I was the man to do the obsequies on John Broderick. He was impressed by the fact that I spelt Jane Austen with an "e" in Austen. It was a little test he had devised to check whether he was in the company of a barbarian.

I had some personal knowledge of Broderick, because I had paid a visit to him once. An unexpected visit. For years, I had harboured a gnawing curiosity about the man who wrote these strange books. Every day, cycling to school along the Ballymahon Road, I would pass the large ornamental gates of his lair, a big old pile hidden away from the world by a spooky forest of trees.

The Broderick family fortune had been founded on Broderick's Bakery, but the boy John had little enough interest in sliced pans and batch loaves, and displayed marked bohemian tendencies. He was certainly the only Athlone man to hang out with the likes of William Burroughs in Tangier, at a time when such things mattered. He had not always been a Flaubertian recluse, and would recall his days of serious drinking, when he might begin a bender in Dublin, and somehow find himself three days later in the wilds of Clare. He wouldn't get into much trouble, as such: he knew what he was doing at the time, but he couldn't quite figure out why the fuck he was doing it.

His books were good enough to be denounced by all right-thinking people of that time, and his isolation was reinforced by a tendency to disguise his characters in a way that made them identifiable only by half the country. If, for example, a priest by the name of Fr Baldwin was having an affair with a local beauty, he might appear in the novel as "Fr Baldwin".

Now in semi-retirement, dividing his time between the old place in Athlone and a residence in Bath, writing some excellent book reviews for the *Irish Times*, he was not to know that a twenty-year-old scribbler, a local boy, was sinking a few pints in the Goldsmith Tavern, figuring that he might pop over for a bit of an oul' chat. Just in case it took another 700 years for an Athlone man to write a novel, The Happy Reaper was coming to call.

All the cliches were in place, the mournful clang of the iron gates, the crunch of the gravel path, the ominous knocking on the great man's door, the eventual appearance of the faithful housekeeper saying "Yes ?", like the old retainer in those Roger Corman movies based on the stories of Edgar Allen Poe.

I made a garbled introduction, and she retired to consult the master. There was mumbling from within, and I could make out the words, "He's Frank Lynch's boy." This seemed to swing it. Mr Broderick received me in a sort of wheelchair, with a rug covering his legs in the manner of a semi-invalid, or a rugby alickadoo on a chilly day in Lansdowne Road. Interior design is not my forte, but this was a drawing room, all right, a drawing room being a sitting room for people with big houses. A large bureau occupied the corner, waiting for its owner to assume the position and draft another masterpiece. Ah, the literary life.

He was nice, almost absurdly gracious, but distinctly fragile, and part of me still wondered if the housekeeper was phoning the Gardai. She brought me coffee. Keeping me there until the squad car arrived? I remember slivers of our conversation. He considered Desmond Hogan, the Ballinasloe novelist, to be a major talent. He was sure that his own books would stand the test of time. Sartre was essentially a man of letters, but Francoise Sagan was the woman for him, if you don't mind. The usual stuff that Athlone lads would be talking about on a slow afternoon.

The poor man got away lightly when you consider that on 'Hanly's People', shortly before he died, he was questioned about his alleged homosexuality. It clearly fazed him, and understandably so. The sexuality of John Broderick, such as it was, seemed to belong to a more spacious era, well before the TV confessional.

If you are wondering who was the last Athlone man to publish a novel, 700 years ago, I'm afraid I can't help you. It was something I picked up while researching the obituary, a clipping from the *Irish Times,* who know about these things. I didn't think that they wrote novels, as such, 700 years ago, but I was prepared to believe it from the *Irish Times*, which knows everything. Was it a bodice-ripper, an airport book, a thriller, a private dick story? "Down these mean cloisters a monk must walk who is not himself mean?" We will never know.

Broderick was a bit exotic, poignant, and heroic, the man who lived in the woods, writing his books. I hope I gave him a good send-off.

Should I mention that Henry Kelly, the game-show king and Pro-Celebrity golfer, spent the early years of his life in Athlone? That Athlone formed the man who made the dramatic transition from being an extremely serious journalist to being the presenter of *Going For Gold?*, and who later quipped that Athlone was a one-horse town without the horse ?

No.

Fuck Henry Kelly. Brian Lenihan and Mary O'Rourke, Athlone's contribution to democracy, will tell you that it is more of a town in the country than a country town, and that if Henry Kelly were to pop over for a round of Celebrity Golf, he would find wonderful things like the Elan Corporation, which seeks to eliminate human illness from the planet, while our army lads are over in the Lebanon, sorting out the Middle East for once and for all. And if he had watched Dick Warner's excellent TV series *Waterways*, he would have seen a place which looks a bit like Venice transplanted to the Irish midlands. Mind you, Dick Warner manages to make most places look like Venice.

A garrison town, the soccer tradition is well established, coming into its own whenever someone called O'Connor is managing The Town. Turlough, Padraig, Michael, anyone called O'Connor, really. Gaelic games are played, of course, but Westmeath in general is known diplomatically as one of "the weaker counties".

THE ALL-IRELAND THEY DON'T TALK ABOUT

I will now tell you something rather tragic about the GAA in Westmeath. I am pretty sure that the last All-Ireland two-in-a-row won by Westmeath, was won by me and a couple of girls. This is not widely known, and perhaps it should not be too widely known, but it's bound to get out sometime, so here we go.

My boyhood connections with the GAA consisted of playing impromptu games of soccer in Pairc Chiarain, which by a Jungian system of inter-connectedness, is adjacent to John Broderick's house. My fellow sporting heretics might include Michael O'Connor, one of the O'Connors who would later play for, and manage, The Town. We were frequently interrupted by a gnarled old caretaker in a Civil War suit who would tell us to feck off over to St Mel's — the Stadium of Light — if we wanted to play that feckin' game. A man of strong Republican leanings, the caretaker once showed us that he meant business by handing around a rubber bullet for our edification. We examined the phallic object gingerly, wondering what the world was coming to.

Nevertheless, on an autumn evening around 1975, I, my sister Caitriona, and one Carmel Foley found ourselves entered in a Quiz in the Pairc Chiarain social centre. We would have no inkling of the amazing tide of events which this harmless night's entertainment would set in train.

We won the Quiz, and discovered that we were now representing the Athlone club in *Scor*, the GAA's extravaganza of culture for the long dark nights after Samhain. *Scor Na N-Og*, to be precise, the Under-16 division. We went on to win the county semi-final and the county final. Now representing Westmeath, we won the Leinster semi-final, despite a legendary GAA administrator sitting in the front row, brazenly prompting the Dublin team, who were too stupid to be helped. We won the Leinster Final on a torrid night in Colaiste Mhuire, and then in Clara, we won the All-Ireland, for fuck's sake.

And then, the following year, we did it all over again. All hail the victorious Westmeath two-in-a-row team !

It was a barrel of laughs all round, being ferried to places like Castletown-Geoghegan and Moate and Athboy, creaming the natives with our smart-aleckery. We even had "mentors", sterling men like Frank Starken and Brother Sebastian, who catered to our every whim, no doubt incandescent at the notion of any outfit from Westmeath shafting the opposition for once in their lives.

Brother Sebastian had a special role as Coach, attending to our Achilles Heel. This was the fact that there was always one round of questions about the GAA, and we knew absolutely nothing about the GAA, so we had to be taught. To this day, my sister and Carmel Foley can probably tell you things about Inky Flaherty and Paddy Ban Brosnan which are known only to the ancients. And my ancestral home is entirely full of GAA plaques and trophies, because we got two of everything, twice over.

Much later, when I was writing articles congratulating Londonderry on bringing the Sam Maguire back to the United Kingdom, jibing and sneering at the Great National Organisation, I would hear of hostile delegates at GAA conventions revealing that the bollocks who writes all that rubbish was happy to take their trophies once upon a time. But it gets worse, much worse. Carmel Foley went on to become the head of the Council for the Status of Women.

THE ACCURSED MEJIA

THE HOT STUFF

When you write for a national paper like the *Sunday Independent*, young people often ask you how they might go about "getting into journalism". This is something of a novelty for me, because when I was writing about groups like Joy Division or Wayne County And The Electric Chairs in *Hot Press*, people would wonder when I was planning to get out of journalism. Up until relatively recently, writing about rock'n'roll was viewed as something of an occult hobby which you would hopefully grow out of, and get a life.

There are as many ways to "get into journalism" as there are ways to fuck up your life in general, and the only one I would not recommend is to win a place at one of our institutes of journalism or communications. Otherwise, you might be a very bright spark with Pulitzer potential who can write like an angel, and two years later, you might emerge saying things like, "Oi'm doing a bit of resurch for Runan Collins at the mument," with a straight face.

One good way to get into journalism is to become homeless for a week, or a fortnight if you can manage it, and write about your experiences. There are certain editors who love this kind of thing, because it takes nerve, and it give them the notion that they can land you with dozens of other dirty jobs that someone has to do. I don't want to assist Right-Wing loonies in any way, but when they give out about the homeless littering the streets, they might float the idea that half of them are trainee journalists working undercover. Today the *Big Issues*, tomorrow *Le Monde*.

If you do it like I did, the first thing you do is acquire a Sex Pistols record, like *God Save The Queen*. This will blow your perception of the cosmos to such a radical degree, that by the time you become a law student, you are already half-way out the door of respectable society. Ideally, your colleagues in Belfield will be such a bunch of hopeless tossers, you will wonder what in the name of jaysus they will be like at forty if they are like this at eighteen, organising "dinner parties" at which they rehearse running the country — dinner parties, of course, being parties with all the good things about parties taken out.

You will make friends with a fellow from Mullingar called John McHugh, and be known by sections of the lawyer community as "Lynch and McHugh, the Reds". McHugh will eventually go to the bad altogether by becoming the producer of the Eurovision in 1995, when Fionnuala Sherry, representing Norway, won yet another Grand Prix for Ireland.

You, meanwhile, will write a deranged "review" of jazz maestro Louis Stewart, whose drummer was smoking a pipe on stage while punk rock raged outside. You will send it to the *Hot Press*, and before you can say "Mary Robinson", you are sitting on a tall stool in Niall Stokes' attic-style office, being offered a job. All you have to do then is get the train down to Athlone in order to explain to your mother that contrary to her reasonable expectations, you are not going to sit in a solicitor's office for the rest of your life trying to soak money out of all and sundry, but instead you have decided to enter what she has every right to regard as the porno industry.

An important departure in your new career is to hitch a lift in Co Clare to the Lisdoonvarna Festival in order to absorb some of the "colour". Your driver will be a middle-aged man in a Toyota who begins to relate his complex sexual history, who offers to take you by the scenic route, and whose hot breath on your neck in the main street of Ballyvaughan forces you to alight at last. The important thing to grasp about journalism is that you begin to regard the possibility of being buggered senseless, beaten to death, and your corpse abandoned in the wilds of Clare as just another 800 words of diamond copy.

The *Hot Press* offices were in Mount Street then, conveniently situated next to the headquarters of Fianna Fail and Fine Gael.The general mood of life on the burning deck of rock journalism is best encapsulated by this question: Why was Liam Mackey running through Newbridge at three in the morning with his shoes in a biscuit tin ?

It was not some sort of Salvador Dali commemoration, just an average production night at the *Hot Press*. He and editor Niall were partaking of the familiar, thrill-seeking ritual known as "following the van", which involved chasing a newspaper delivery vehicle at high speed through the Irish night, catching up with it at, perhaps, Monasterevin, and handing over a package of the sacred pages for eventual collection in Tralee by the printers, *The Kerryman*.

On this night, the pursuit became more entertaining than usual, when the wretched Stokesmobile ran out of petrol in Newbridge. Mackey sought help, or perhaps asylum, at the nearby Garda HQ, where he was directed to a filling station up the road. The best that the Gardai could offer by way of a petrol-container was a biscuit tin. By now, the heavens had thrown down a monsoon, and haste being of the essence, the resourceful Mackey decided that his splendid new white slip-on shoes were surplus to requirements, so he popped them in the tin, and proceeded to the filling station hot-foot, as it were.

And that is why Liam Mackey was running through Newbridge at three in the morning with his shoes in a biscuit tin.

On such nights of sin, with the law being broken on a minute-to-minute basis, it would have taken a mighty leap of the imagination to visualise a day when Niall might succeed Judge Seamus Henchy to anything at all. His prospects of a seat on the

Supreme Court were negligible, and as far as we know, Judge Henchy has never been party to a record entitled 'Gobble Gobble Hey!', or issued vehement demands for the legalisation of hashish. Yet today, Niall bestrides the Independent Radio and Television Commission, easing himself into the good judge's still-warm saddle.

If the stewardship of the independent radio sector requires an intimate awareness of impending disaster on an almost daily basis, then N Stokes is the right man for the job. In the early phases of *Hot Press*, he embraced mayhem and horror as close friends which perversely fuelled his vision of "keeping Ireland safe for rock'n'roll". The abyss may have been reached with a fund-raising gig at Punchestown, one of the few known examples of a benefit concert which reported an impressive financial loss. It was less a case of Self Aid than Self Immolation, yet it seemed to merely strengthen his mad resolve to nurse his bawling baby to health. The magazine which refused to die is now a sturdy teenager, though some of its contributors are starting to go to bed a lot earlier.

Even its misprints tended to have a happy ending. Chris de Burgh was once listed as playing the "RDS Humping Arena", while Brian Behan, who had described himself as "a total workaholic", took it in good part when he became "a total alcoholic" in print. I once led people to believe that U2 had signed up to Jan Floor's Wasted Trousers Agency, when in fact they had signed to Ian Foulkes' Wasted Talent Agency. Somehow, they survived. And anyway, I prefer Jan Floor's Wasted Trousers Agency.

Niall's unending drive to liberate us from the thrall of priest-craft and obscurantism, finds fortnightly expression in his editorials, a compendium of which might well be headlined, POP EDITOR CALLS ON POPE TO RESIGN.

Once, on a slow night, he took umbrage with the aerospace industry over a recent spate of aviation disasters, prompting Eamonn McCann to remark, "I see that Niall Stokes is totally opposed to plane crashes." An apostle of sexual liberation, as well as IRTC chairman, it is tempting to imagine him sending a helpful memo to RTE, suggesting a shift in the orientation of its daytime radio schedule: "Begin with Morning Sex, then on to the Gay Sex Show, and through to The Sex At One. Continue with Marian Finucane's Live Sex, and finally Sex At Five with Myles Dungan."

He might tell the "independents" that it would be an idea to honour perhaps a fraction of the shameless commitments which they made to the IRTC during those farcical public hearings — the restoration of Irish as a living tongue within six months, and other such bolloxology. Before Charlie Haughey effed and blinded his way into immortality, a fateful *Hot Press* interview with Michael D Higgins began the magazine's policy of talking to politicians and actually printing what they said. In the intervening years, few could sleep easy lest they be rung up and asked what music they like to listen to when they are "making love", or how often they have smoked cannabis, or what they would do if they discovered that their son was gay.

Your present corespondent was once despatched to ask Brian Lenihan, *inter alia*, what he thought about AIDS. I decided that Brian would reckon that it should be avoided at all costs, and that Fianna Fail categorically believed it should be avoided at all costs. So I spared him the pain.

Now that people are asking Niall hard questions, he must be as forthright about radio as he is about plane crashes. Meanwhile, Liam Mackey is looking like a cert for Ceann Comhairle.

It may surprise a lot of readers to learn that the majority of Irish journalists are fairly intelligent people who, on the whole, prefer a good story to be partially accurate, and who stand their round. Some of them are even concerned at the adverse effect that their writings might have. I, for example, probably prolonged Georgie Best's marriage by a few weeks due to a totally selfless act.

I saw him at Dublin Airport with his then wife Angie, looking like a million dollars in a beautiful white suit. And Angie looked pretty good as well. I had seen them the previous night on the *Late Late Show*, when Angie said that she would leave the great man if he touched another drop of alcohol. Then, as I sat in a window-seat for the flight to London, I saw Georgie and Angie coming down the aisle. And then Georgie sat down beside me, with Angie on the outside.

This, I thought, is one for the grandchildren, to be sure.

It was horns-of-a-dilemma time. There was an enormous temptation to blurt out a greeting, to compliment the man in the white suit on his genius. But reader, I refrained. I figured that every loo-lah who had ever sat beside Georgie Best on a plane had invaded his privacy to some degree, and certainly every loo-lah journalist. But I did something else for which there will be a crown awaiting me in a better world. When the hostess asked me if I would care for a drop of brandy, or maybe something stronger, I said "No." I said "No thanks, ma'am, not for me, thank you very much." I sacrificed a free drink so that Georgie wouldn't get the smell of a cork, and be gripped by the ancient urge to join me for a tincture. Matt Talbot can kiss my ass.

Journalists actually pay for their drink from time to time, and can often be seen huddled in bars, issuing forth guffaws of raucous hysterical laughter, sharing their experiences like a group of people who suffer from an unusual illness. And journalism, I feel, is primarily a form of illness.

The symptoms include a childish obsession with things which are of absolutely no interest to the general public, but which gladden the journalistic heart regardless. A good opening blast is considered to be something of an art-form, the pinnacle of which was John Waters' opener to a piece on Fossett's Circus: "The first time this reporter saw an elephant, it was coming out of a pub. It was the elephant who was coming out of the pub for a change, and not the reporter", it went. True enough, he had a photograph of a circus elephant coming out of a pub in Castlerea, as a publicity stunt. Hacks have been known to weep openly at such perfection.

Great headlines also quicken the journalistic pulse, particularly The Ones That Got Away. No heart is so heavy as that of the headline-writer who has to spike the perfect headline on grounds of taste and decorum. There should be a little plot in Glasnevin, the Tomb Of The Unknown Headline, for beauties which didn't make it: I KNEW MCBRIDE WHEN HE USED TO ROCK'N'ROLL on an obituary of Sean McBride. Never made it. HONEY I SHAGGED THE KIDS on a Michael Jackson article. Never made it. A jockey is neutered in a stable accident: AND THEY'RE OFF! Never made it.

One outrage of political incorrectness which actually made it was a tiny piece on page three of the *Evening Press*, a snippet about free bus travel in New Zealand for the partners of gay employees. QUARES PLEASE was the headline.

It is such paltry amusements which bring a little frisson of joy to an otherwise trying trade. Such titbits are as naught compared to the raw meat demanded by the hounds of Wapping and their trans-Atlantic counterparts. The upright citizens of Irish journalism are often left in mute astonishment when Wapping's Finest arrive in town, mob-handed in their endless quest for The Truth. Or The Facts, which is not the same thing at all. It may be The Truth about the sex-life of Chris De Burgh, but by the cut of their jib, you would think that the future of civilised life on this planet depended on it. They all appear to be called Rob, and they think nothing of staking out a love-nest for forty-eight hours, pissing into McDonalds' cartons for fear of missing that photograph.

They in turn will regard themselves as public service stiffs on the Reithian model by comparison with the American tabloids. This, ladies and gentlemen, is The Hard Stuff.

THE HARD STUFF

CRIPPLE SELLS HUMP TO BUTCHER — FAMILY POISONED BY HUNCHBURGER [US tabloid headline]. It seems to have escaped the attention of most of the world's media that John F Kennedy recently met with Bill Clinton at Camp David. Now elderly and crippled, but surprisingly energetic, JFK scolded Clinton for his indecisiveness, and said of Hillary, "Ask not what your husband can do for you, ask what you can do for your husband."

So now we know, thanks to *Weekly World News*, the great American tabloid, which illustrates its scoop with a grainy photo of Clinton pushing a white-haired JFK around the grounds in a wheelchair. It further reveals that Kennedy, who has been quietly living in Europe since he sustained massive injuries in the attempted assassination, has had secret meetings with Presidents Nixon, Ford, Carter, Reagan and Bush.

While *WWN* makes *The Sun* look like the *Herald Tribune*, it also puts your average British tabloid to shame with the unalloyed purity of its vision. The muck-rakers on this side of the Atlantic are still encumbered by the tyranny of "facts", a condition with which they are uncomfortable, but which they endure in a misplaced attempt at a credibility which they will never attain. Despite their brazen front, British tabloids will spoil excellent stories about flying saucers and werewolves, and the current whereabouts of Elvis, with sombre political commentary, and even some twisted shite about the economy.

You might think that a *Sun* editorial headlined SHOVE IT UP YOUR BOTTOM, JACQUES ! is not especially sombre, but it is in the Edmund Burke league compared to the uninhibited chutzpah of *WNN* and other true poets of the grungeloid muse. Like the three great pillars of their wisdom — JFK, Elvis, and Marilyn — they are unshackled by mortal constraints, soaring through the firmament of the paranormal and the superhuman, and with the pictures to prove it.

MOM GIVES BIRTH TO FIFTEEN BABIES — AT ONE TIME; WOLF
SERENADES TOWN BY HOWLING AMAZING GRACE; SKINNY
HUSBAND SMOTHERED BY 300-POUND WIFE'S BOOBS; ALIENS
CONSIDER EARTH THE GHETTO OF THE UNIVERSE; ELVIS IS NOT
DEAD — I JUST TALKED TO HIM ON THE PHONE; JESUS' FACE
APPEARS IN DISHWASHER.

All of these wonderful, at times deeply moving stories, are
supported by eye-witness accounts, by pictorial evidence, or by
the opinion of eminent, if unconventional, thinkers. We can
clearly see the face of Jesus Christ etched onto a tumbler in the
dishwasher, giving the story a bit more provenance than those
sightings of St Anthony on various domestic appliances in
Artane, or of statues shimmying in Co Cork. He looks a bit like
a member of The Eagles.

Most impressive, though, is the way that *WNN* enlists the
views of experts such as Dr Dainik Bhavan, a "renegade
Professor" based in Calcutta, whose shocking study reveals that
GETTING CAUGHT IN THE RAIN MAKES YOU STUPID. Dr Bhavan
always felt that there was a link between heavy rainfall and
lapses in mental power. Now his researches have proved him
correct.

The inspirational thing about the great American tabloid is
that it concentrates on those who have been truly marginalised
by society. Not the poor, or the oppressed, or members of Young
Fine Gael, but those who are genuinely on the outer fringes. Dead
people, for example, live again in the pages of *WNN*, sometimes
assisting with the fine-tuning of U.S. foreign policy. Women who
weigh over 300 stones will always find a sympathetic ear. And
there is usually a *cead mile failte* on the mat for visitors from
foreign planets.

There is ample room for the maverick, like Hiram Grale, 86,
who got his 84-year-old girlfriend, Franny, pregnant, and was
forced to marry her at shotgun-point by her papa, Alvers Hopper,
102. "Anyone who gets my little girl in trouble better make an

honest woman out of her, or I'm gonna put a hole clean through him," Hopper fumed.

There is only the occasional lapse into the moralistic cant favoured by the hounds of Wapping. A cannibal is due to be released from the "nut-house", and readers are asked to decide whether (a) *"They should lock up this maniac in jail and let him rot there. He shouldn't be allowed out for five minutes no matter how much he whines about not seeing his relatives — he'd probably just try to murder and eat them." Or (b) "It wasn't his fault that he killed and ate a perfectly innocent boy. Let him go free — but only if he promises not to murder and eat anyone else."*

I detect a certain slant to this, but I'm sure that *WWN* readers will not allow their judgement to be clouded by sentiment. These are people who, on a weekly basis, confront cosmic truths of eternal resonance, like WE CAN'T FLUSH AWAY THE GHOST IN OUR TOILET. There is a picture of the bowl, featuring a man's ethereal visage engulfed with flames which may never be extinguished by the fluids of mortal beings. He too has his story.

"Do you think that YOU BASTARDS! *is too short for a Leader Column?"* [Line from a satirical play about tabloid journalism].

One would usually be very hard-pressed to invoke the remotest comparison between Kelvin McKenzie, editor of *The Sun*, and the distinguished American scribe, H L Mencken. But during McKenzie's appearance before a House of Commons Committee, called to investigate the debaucheries of the Press, he embodied Mencken's dictum that the relationship between the journalist and the politician should ideally be akin to that which pertains between the dog and the lamp-post.

He is pathologically reticent about personal publicity, so the great and the good gathered around him must have anticipated a thorough mauling of him and his inexcusably vile organ. Instead, millions of TV viewers witnessed the suave Committee members being reduced to mush by a performance of expertly-pitched belligerence on the part of Lord Kelv of Wapping. Addressing them as "you people", he induced a collective squirm in the body language of his tormentors.

"You people" would prefer an American system? In America, he could print the names and sexual peccadilloes of every MP client of Miss Whiplash, and no-one could claim a single penny in damages. *"You people"* must be nuts. *"You people"* complain about offering a fiver to *Sun* readers who make a sighting of Camilla Parker-Bowles. It's just a bit of fun, you old jossers. Don't you understand fun? *"You people"* say that Camilla is just an ordinary person? She is sleeping with the future King of England behind her husband's back, and you think this is ordinary?

And on and on.

At last, the monstrous legend of Kelvin McKenzie had reached a mass audience. Here is a fanatical tabloid loyalist who referred to *The Guardian* as "the world's worst", and who genuinely believes that the broadsheets, or "Unpopulars", carry long articles because the writers are incapable of producing concise, crisp, copy of the kind which adorns the good old Currant Bun. A rabid workaholic and martinet, he once saw an employee raving incoherently to himself in a corner. On being challenged, the employee said that he was sure Kelvin was going to give him a bollocking, so he thought he'd save him the bother.

Here is the author of GOTCHA!, *The Sun*'s version of the *Belgrano* sinking, and disastrously, of THE TRUTH, which erroneously claimed that the corpses of Liverpool fans at Hillsborough had been pickpocketed. He will still swear that every *Sun* story is "101% accurate", despite his propensity for putting more "spin" on a piece than Jack Nicklaus with his trusty wedge. "Spin" is a *Sun* reporter covering the Air India disaster by ringing up every nautical official in Ireland until he found one who would tell him that there are sharks in these parts. Completely tame sharks, but sharks nonetheless.

"Spin" is *The Sun* reporting the findings of a survey which put English children at the bottom of a European educational table, under the headline, WE'RE THICKER THAN THE IRISH.

McKenzie passionately despises the "on the one hand, and on the other hand" school of Unpopular journalism, a philosophy summed up during the latter, barmy days of Thatcher, when he mused, "She's wrong, but she's strong." His hyperactivity was once cleverly exploited by a financial reporter who wanted to run a hate-campaign against a mandarin of The City. Knowing that the complexities would bore Kelvin within about thirty seconds, he explained that the guy must go, "because he's a cunt". — "Alright, then, if he's a cunt, we'll go after him."

His devotion to the imperishable *Sun* reader has led him to adopt an unnaturally yobbish turn of phrase, and a level of scatology which makes Charlie Haughey's *Hot Press* interview sound like a parson conducting Evensong. The same *Sun* reader, who — he fulminated to the Commons Committee — was not being extended the same rights as the Royal Family, who are allowed private hearings.

The proceedings would doubtless have been conducted in a far more gracious and congenial fashion with the editor of *The Times*, or any of the other Unpopulars, on the stand. But it would have been a case of like meeting like, arriving at a flaccid gentleman's agreement. The twisted magnificence of McKenzie's tirade re-stated some fundamental adversarial principles. The fact that it was left up to Lord Kelv of Wapping to enunciate these home truths, suggests that English newspapers may be in more of a mess than they realise.

The Sun is now general all over Ireland. Kelvin nicknamed the Irish edition "The Diddley", as in diddley-aye. Gord 'elp us.

This reporter is aware of certain incidents involving a well-known Irish political person which, if made public and given the right amount of "spin", would almost certainly damage his career beyond redemption. These incidents in no way affect his public duties, and do not involve any injury to third parties. They merely feature this person behaving like an almighty berk. Nor is there any sustained pattern of berkdom in this man's behaviour. But given the proper tabloid treatment, he would be a national laughing stock, and his life effectively ruined.

It occurred to me too that I am aware of certain incidents involving myself which, translated into a full-blown *Sun*-style format, wouldn't do a whole lot of good for my career either. And I am sure that the vast majority of people reading this can probably recall a few incidents which would not bear the scrutiny of the paparazzi without considerable damage to all their careers.

In the case of the political person, it would be grotesquely unfair to expose this isolated indiscretion, but in a pure tabloid sense, it doesn't have to be fair, it only has to be factual. TV personality Frank Bough is "found on" at an exotic torture chamber, a sequel to the discovery that he was given to passing the evening in the company of "vice girls", snorting Colombian Marching Powder. This had no harmful effect on his work as a TV presenter, and held out no bad example to the young, because we know that Frank sometimes went straight from his coke parties to front Breakfast TV with remarkable lucidity for a man in his condition. That he maintained such avuncular command of the medium, knowing where he had just been, is both admirable and hilarious.

To nail a man for his sexual unorthodoxy is unfair and vindictive, since Bough has never proselytised either for or against whips, chains, thumbscrews, what have you. His marital and drugs problems are his own affair. Yet there is a cruel humour about the whole business which the tabloids will cite in self-justification.

And they will be right. They will be utter Bastards but they will be right.

Tabloidese is a participative blood-sport in which the readers are as complicit as the layout artist. Yea, even the *Guardian* reader who begrudges Rupert Murdoch 25p. but who leafs furtively through *The Sun* to keep abreast of the Royal frenzy is ensuring that the personal tragedies of people like Frank Bough will continue to get the treatment.

It is not widely understood just how volatile the tabloid market can be. After its nauseating coverage of the Hillsborough disaster, its Elton John cock-up, and other misjudgements, *The Sun*'s sales figures took a serious and apparently permanent hammering. Despite those colossal sales-figures, the tabloids live on a precipice, and if they lose their touch, the readers will be as fickle as the papers themselves are, in lionising Boy George or Gazza and then shafting them.

Nor is it widely understood that to maintain that touch requires exceptional skill and intuition, not necessarily for the Lowest Common Denominator, but for the LCD that millions of people will happily swallow. There is a big difference, as the Hillsborough debacle demonstrated.

They have correctly deduced that the only discernible function of the Royal Family is to provide amusement to the masses, of any kind whatsoever, regardless of the methods by which such amusement is transmitted. Reassurance too, in the sense that such an awful family offers hope and comfort to all. The methods — hidden cameras, eavesdropping on phone conversations, bribing employees — are completely reprehensible, but they rely on the readers to be like football fans who don't care about the tactics as long as they get the right result.

Like Al Capone, the tabloids provide a service, and their destruction must ultimately be self-inflicted. As for the readers, let he who is without *Sun*...

In this rancid atmosphere, a new buzz-word has entered the lexicon of public debate in Ireland — "tabloidisation". In a strange echo of the Fifties, when the *Catholic Standard* was railing against the threat posed to our civilisation by smutty rags like *The People*, the decent men and women at the coal-face of Irish journalism are being urged not to go down the Wapping road.

Since the British tabloids have already put down firm roots in the public consciousness, over-sexed and over here, the argument veers into the nebulous area of national pride, with Irish newspapers assuming a touching role as the last bastion of media Christianity, a beacon which shines through the barbarian fog. Amid dramatic rumours of crack teams of muck-rakers skulking through the undergrowth of Irish politics and religion, feeding their gross appetites on the sexual misadventures of our great leaders, the fear exists that in the battle for circulation, we will go down to their level.

It is all very sad.

There is a grand wee double standard at work here, a very traditional one whereby we blame the Brits for corrupting us, despite much evidence that we are only dying to be corrupted. Hundreds of thousands of Irish people buy the British scandal-sheets, not because Rupert Murdoch is putting something in the water, but presumably because they enjoy this species of tripe.

What we have here is one of those Human Nature problems.

Ashen-faced scribes will lament the case of Sir Peter Harding, big in the British Army, and Lady Buck, who has big tits, and express outrage at the fact that the *News of The World* now decides who runs the British Army. Yet they will be lying to you, my friends, because they will have reached this pitch of outrage long after they have gone through the normal range of reactions, from amusement through to hilarity, with a touch of "There, but for the grace of God..."

This was a true cracker of the tabloid muse. The toff and the scarlet woman. Make that two toffs and the scarlet woman. The head of the British Army hopelessly in love and there's a war going on. Crack headlines like SIR ANTONY WAS A DRUNKEN

VIOLENT OLD FOOL WHO TOOK TWO YEARS TO CONSUMMATE OUR MARRIAGE. Lashings of soft porn from the boudoir of Buck, interspersed with pure slapstick like *"Sir Peter jumped naked from her bed, mumbling: Must go — top level conference on!"*

Then there was the utterly brazen hypocrisy of the *NOTW* claiming that they were forced into these disclosures because Sir Hard-On posed a security risk, along with some heinous gibberish about Iraqi spies. Here, the readers smirk conspiratorially, and wonder why the *NOTW* is worried about this when it is spending a fortune luring him into entrapment, rather than keeping it hush-hush in the national interest. An important strand of the conspiracy with its readers is that it prints this stuff with deep regret. It damn near breaks their bloody hearts.

But let us scotch this cant about the *News Of The World* deciding who runs the British Army. Since it is the great unwashed who read the *NOTW* that will be doing all the fighting and dying for the British Army, it is arguable that they should be choosing the top man in the first place.

The growth of the tabloid culture was always an abomination to the British establishment, because it heightened their visibility, and made them more accessible to the plebs. The sex scandal is a great leveller, making figures of fun out of a ruling elite which places a premium on not being found out. Between the sheets, the mystique is removed, and the Tory Minister or the Army General resigns because he has been reduced to human size. His reputation for chasing skirt just like any groping Joe has caused too much sniggering in the ranks.

In this country, the territory is quite different, and when people anticipate an avalanche of erotic revelations from Kildare Street, they are not comparing like with like. Here, we are on more familiar terms with the mighty, and view them with little deference. We know them on a human level. We live down the road from them, and accept their perversions with a neighbourly grace. I doubt if we would be particularly inflamed unless there was genuine weirdness involved, some angle of brutality, someone, as they say, doing the dog on it entirely.

A haymaker of a sex scandal is more likely to emanate from the Church, which still sells a line of lofty mystique. As for the jeremiahs of the respectable mejia, the attitude to their squalid tabloid brethren is redolent of the line that an alcoholic is someone you don't like who drinks more than you. In all their virtue, you will probably find that they will drop in, "only for the one".

The tabloid filleting of Chris De Burgh could be regarded as a fair cop, guv, but society is to blame. The wandering minstrel told Gerry Ryan that he had been contacted by several "serious people, top people", who said, "There, but for the grace of God..."

It struck me that Irish tabloid fever is still at a relatively low pitch compared to the British type, not through the lack of material generated by "serious people, top people", but because we lack a creature called Max Clifford to facilitate the flow of scandal. Nominally a "publicist", Max is a poet of the tabloid muse, a man who has dedicated his life to parlaying sleaze into entertainment into money, who can turn the dreariest dalliance into a well-turned epic, each stanza honed to the last syllable down to the deathless pay-off line.

Here, we might have regarded the De Burgh love fiasco as a little local difficulty. It was his international stardom which lured Wapping's Finest onto the trail. The little local difficulties which have afflicted Irish show-business legends throughout the ages have not taken off into the tabloid stratosphere, even though they would make for world-class models of the genre.

There is one man who knows where the bodies are buried, one man who could make Max Clifford reach for his cheque-book with trembling hands, his hair standing on end as though by electrocution. This man is even a journalist. He works for a tabloid newspaper. He is a member of my Union. Significantly, he is also a priest.

Fr Brian D'Arcy, confessor to the Irish show band and cabaret industries, has heard some ripping yarns in his time, I'll warrant. We will take it for granted that on an ordinary night, the average show band would have broken all Ten Commandments, including the one forbidding the murder of totally innocent songs. But what of the extraordinary exotica, the orgies, the under-age sex, the one who likes to cover his women in blue paint, the one who ties them to a door-knob, the one who preserves locks of their pubic hair in a mattress?

Consider the paroxysms of moral agony in which Fr Brian must have writhed, as he juggled his priestly vows with his sacred calling as a tabloid journalist? If he had not been such a kind person, and had become instead Max Clifford just for one day, the roof of Mount Argus would have gone up in the time it takes Big Tom to sing "when the hue wears off of your crystal chandeliers".

I think that the old reliables of the ballroom and cabaret circuits have evaded the full tabloid treatment out of a peculiar sense of the national interest rather than the moral interest. They are such a part of what we are, that to have printed their excesses was tantamount to embroiling the entire nation in a conspiracy of perversion.

In the Max Clifford era, there is a moral dimension, of sorts. It is arguable that merely being of interest to the tabloids makes a performer's protests morally unsustainable. There was a time not so long ago when people in the general territory of "rock" were mostly absent from the mainstream media, a time when the majority of thick *Sun* readers could not name a member of, say, Led Zeppelin, suspecting only that they were hairy degenerates who played far too loud, had sinister mansions in the country, and who consorted with German witches in sick occult ceremonies.

The sundering of the connection between rock and the "counter-culture", the urge towards respectability as epitomised by De Burgh, the maudlin drives to save the world, and the emergence of the rock-band-as-multinational-corporation, have turned the rock industry into something as banal as a daytime soap. It is full of anodyne, arse-licking, cabaret merchants, to the extent that if Max Clifford is looking for a bit of decent hedonism, he must consult the register of Tory MPs, military big-shots, and judges. It looks as though the spirit of rock'n'roll is being kept alive by the Right Honourable Alan Clark MP, while De Burgh lines out with Dame Vera Lynn and Bob Hope on board the QE2, conduct that would once have been regarded by his peers as beyond the Pale.

Our user-friendly rock stars are delighted when their dodgy press releases are puffed by *The Sun*, making them visible to millions of mug punters, forgetting that the same mug punters are going to be interested in their antics off the park, and that if you live by the tabloid, you will die by the tabloid, every time. So taking it from first principles, a lot of the glitterati get burned, basically, because they are crap.

That is the moral of the story, and as Max Clifford will tell you for free, there's a lot of it about.

Thus, as Ireland came to terms with its first live political sex scandal, it was as though the opinion-formers of the nation had discovered, not just the scandal, but sex itself. Losing their virginity in this area, they just couldn't stop talking about it. And how appropriate that the great event took place in furtive circumstances in the Phoenix Park. Virginities, on the whole, tend to be lost in such inglorious circumstances, and a lot of people would prefer to draw a discreet veil over the ambiance of what short-story writers refer to as one's "sexual awakening".

Emmett Stagg was just a facilitator in a process whereby all branches of the media, the political class, and the public at large, tried to come to terms with this unwieldy new phenomenon in their lives. With much beating of breasts and examining of consciences, we each dealt with it in our own way, aware of how painful it all was, of course, but unable to stop yapping about it, and hoping that the next episode would be conducted in more auspicious circumstances. Stephen's Green, perhaps, or even a cheap hotel room on the Northside.

The papers which made the initial penetration might as well have been issuing invitations to a gang-bang, as RTE radio in particular launched itself into a spinning frenzy the like of which has not been seen since Eamonn Casey did the dirt, and Annie Murphy arrived among us with her gossamer wings. It was dizzy stuff, as Gaybo, Pat Kenny, Gerry Ryan, the News At One, and Marian Finucane all led with a dissertation on the meaning of it all.

Some praised the *Irish Times* for not printing the original story. I suggest that the next ad campaign for the Old Lady of D'Olier Street should read thus: "We sat on the Casey scandal until it burned the skin off our bottoms. We were aloof on the Phoenix Park affair. The *Irish Times* — not so much a newspaper, more a state of mind." With celibacy no longer an option, its policy of safe sex extended to a wonderfully solemn editorial involving "the supposed activities of so-called 'rent boys'", echoing Marian Finucane's enquiry into cruising, straight from the cruiser's mouth.

On the political front, the expressions of sympathy for Emmett Stagg could be regarded as genuine, but were heavily laden with the unspoken dread, "There, but for the grace of God..." They issued comical warnings that the Irish media must not descend to the level of their guttersnipe English counterparts, exposing every illicit ejaculation, regardless of context. They can relax for a while, the poor babies, because we in the Irish media are basically wonderful people who do not yet consider it a matter of public interest that a politician is having it off with someone other than his or her spouse.

There has to be a secondary element, a clear contradiction between the politician's public utterances and private behaviour.

So if there are any fornicating Fianna Fail fathers-of-seven out there, with a strong line on the Sanctity of the Family, I suggest that they re-consider their position, like immediately.

The problem with the Stagg story is that it just barely contained this secondary element, namely, its proximity to prostitution. Emmett Stagg is a progressive, pluralist person, who has never pontificated on matters of sexual morality. Hypocrisy was not the issue here, just the sense that he had been an unmerciful eejit, all things considered. The legs of this story also needed strengthening because it lacked one crucial element of a good old sex scandal in the grand tradition.

It was not funny. Or at least not funny enough. It had none of the riotous hilarity of the Casey fiasco, and it was bereft of the exotic paraphernalia which accompanies a Tory blockbuster — plastic bags, women's stockings, mandarin oranges, football jerseys, rubber handcuffs, shotguns, one-legged porno actresses, glamourous call-girls and Russian spies, and all of that mighty raft of detail which elevates a mere sexual episode to the pantheon of the absurd.

Casting around for some light humour, I noted that the players in this over-extended drama included politicians by the name of Stagg and Cox, and a journalist named Balls. Stagg, Cox, and Balls. 'Twas fate that brought them together.

But a word-gag is not enough, hence the frantic spinning on the airwaves, as frustrations were worked out on such a forlorn target. They were not so much sorry for Emmett Stagg as sorry for themselves, wondering whether it's all it's cracked up to be, this sex-scandal racket. Nor was the fact of homosexual activity per se enough to inflame the Irish public, displaying a refreshing maturity in its old age.

That man Casey may have spoiled us for life.

As South Africa prepared for its first democratic elections, RTE shouldered the white man's burden with a vengeance. They didn't so much send a team to cover the South African election as mount an expedition. With the finest minds of Montrose enmeshed in the Eurovision trauma, it was as though the Current Affairs crew demanded their own mega-bash, with all hands on board.

For its troubles, this tortured land found itself playing host to Charlie Bird, John Bowman, Sean O'Rourke, John Egan, Bryan Dobson, Mike Milotte, and technical personnel too numerous to mention. It must have been touch-and-go as to whether Ronan Collins was out and about in Pretoria instead of Punchestown. 'Both Sides Now', with Paschal Mooney linking up to Kwazulu province, would have been a fine thing too.

In this game of "Let's play at being CNN", Sean O'Rourke, keen as mustard, spoke to Joe Duffy on 'Soundbyte' to let him know how the expedition was progressing. It was a sort of talking postcard, and only to be expected in the context of the general ballyhoo. There was much re-iteration of the theme that we were living through important moments in history, and thanks to RTE, we were not left short of historians. To assist the South Africans as they strive to obey the civilities which we in the Free World cherish, 'Questions & Answers' came from Johannesburg. Or rather, it went to Johannesburg.

Though a million miles away from home, there was something reassuringly familiar about the thrust and tenor of the proceedings. Reassuring in a disturbing sort of way. From right to left, the panelists were our own Kader Asmal; Sheila Camerer of the National Party; General Olesegun Olessanjo of Kenya; and Peter Oucamp of the Afrikaaner Volksfront.

We were unlikely to hear *ráiméis* from holidaying Irish politicians, who used to come back with pained eulogies about "this beautiful country", to which one could only reply, "scenery is not the issue here". Visually, the man who says he is the General, one of Kenya's most notoriously peaceful men, was a magnificent creature, whose traditional robes were an obvious departure from the standard 'Q & A' dress code.

For one brief horrible moment, when Jonathan Livingstone Bowman invited questions from the audience, I feared that the camera would sweep across the usual suspects, flown out from Montrose to accompany the expedition, asking the panel what they thought about the Stagg controversy, or how they relate to toxic emissions in Cork Harbour. Mercifully, it was a normal South African audience, albeit with an unusual Irish flavour. They were not as contrary as their Dublin counterparts, in spite of their suffering.

Once it settled down, an eerie sense of recognition began to creep into the occasion. I think it was the Afrikaaner Volksfront fellow who started it off, talking a lot about "the right to self-determination", of which we hear a great deal. In modern parlance, "the right to self-determination" translates as the right of wretched little Nazis to kill people in pursuit of a garbled destiny. This chap reminded me for some reason of Latka in the comedy series 'Taxi'. Latka's mannerisms with Louie's personality.

We could have been back in Dublin blathering about the North, with the three fairly democratic people united against the wild man, thinking it's a pity you can't lock him up, but you have to talk to him, because he's probably not the worst of them, total wanker though he is. Soon we were very much at home, knowing exactly what everyone was going to say. Our own Kader Asmal's views are exhaustively well-known on all salient matters, the National Party woman was hard but fair, like a Pee Dee beamed over to Jo'burg, and the General, plugging away in the neutral corner, just wanted a better world.

Kader's years in Ireland did not go to waste, because he appeared, incongruously, like a Fianna Fail person, sporting a green-and-yellow rosette, and boasting that the only thing to be decided is who finishes second, third, fourth, and fifth. The audience was too cultured to yelp "Yahoo!" This encouraged Sheila Camerer to fill the room with bullshit by declaring that the National Party is going to win an overall majority, like the Pee Dees sizing up their excellent candidates and forecasting a landslide.

Yes, it was bullshit, but optimistic bullshit is what South Africa needs to smother the likes of Peter Oucamp and his ugly friends. 'Questions & Answers' contribution was to open another small pipeline for the stuff, as RTE entered the business of colonial expansion.

One of the problems encountered by RTE as it competes with tatty stations owned by Rupert Murdoch, is that it is obliged to cover events, not because they are entertaining, or exciting, or even vaguely interesting, but because they are there. They are further obliged to cover them in Irish.

Thus it was that Eamonn Lawlor, David Hanly, Una Claffey, Shane McElhatton, and Tommie Gorman, made the tedious journey to Cannes for an EU Summit. Tommie's journey was perhaps the least tedious, because he is an old Euro-hand, who probably knows the mainland of Europe well enough to take a few short-cuts. The others had to haul themselves away from the best Irish weather in living memory, and shuffle off to the Riviera. On our behalf. Because we demand it. Because it is there.

It was clear that David Hanly was not having a wonderful time when he kicked off 'Morning Ireland' from a Cannes where there was "brilliant sunshine and uncomfortable heat". Ah yes. It looks good on the telly, but the oul' humidity is a killer. Throw in the thousands of other journalists and broadcasters trying to perform their public service remit, and you have a sticky old situation all round. Wall-to-wall public service in the sweltering Mediterranean.

Twice, Hanly stated the consensus that it would be a dull Summit. John Palmer of *The Guardian* agreed that there was "a certain dullness". A Danish journalist said that the next Summit in Spain would be just as dull, due to Filipe Gonzalez' domestic problems, and the one after that in Italy would be dull, because they change their governments the way other people change their neckties. The one after that, in Ireland, will be more exciting. Up to a point.

Thus, for the sake of a sound-byte about "de-commissioning", and some speculation about the parlous future of John Major, RTE had to despatch half-a-dozen of its heavy hitters to the Riviera. Who says that RTE is cutting corners on its Current Affairs output ? Bring them to me, and I'll fight them.

There was yet another RTE person, of sorts, in the shape of Shane Kenny, who "went over to the other side", and became the Government Press Secretary. He must endure one dull Summit after another, while perfecting the ancient Press Secretary technique of "lurking discreetly in the background". At least he is spared the trials of his erstwhile colleagues, who have to position themselves in front of a harbour full of big yachts, saying things like, *"Cannes is normally associated with the glamour of the film industry, but today the attention was focussed on Europe's top politicians"* ...you know yourself.

Their consolation was that thousands of other public servants were saying the same thing, only in foreign languages, with different yachts in the background. Meanwhile, the film-stars have moved to Ireland, where the action is.

The most striking image of this dull Summit was that of Douglas Hurd swimming in the sea. The retiring Douglas can do that sort of thing now, without *The Sun* plastering it over the front page, and the headline, WAVING OR DROWNING? It's all behind him now, this yoke of public service. He can swim wherever he likes.

The Cannes Summit reached this conclusion: Douglas Hurd is free at last, free at last, Lord God Almighty, he is free at last.

So is Olivia O'Leary. The announcement, when it came, was almost coy. In that peculiarly stilted style of the straight 'News' bulletin, where the average viewer is presumed to have arrived from Saturn just before the show, Peter Finnerty told us that "the broadcaster Olivia O'Leary" had resigned from 'Prime Time' for personal and professional reasons.

There was a picture of the broadcaster Olivia O'Leary to illustrate the item, and to clarify that this was not Olivia O'Leary the champion weight-lifter, or Olivia O'Leary the astronaut. Then there was an ad-break, during which one was bound to speculate on the nature of these personal and professional reasons, somewhat peeved at RTE's implication that this was for them to know and for us to find out.

On a personal level, there was always the possibility that Olivia had developed a rare form of creeping whiplash after years of tilting her head at an awkward angle and saying, "Now, if I may turn to you, Brian Cowen". There was nothing to assist us with our enquiries. The BBC is in a state of some upheaval due to the lunatic bureaucracies inspired by Director-General John Birt, but Birt will still present himself on 'Newsnight' to evade whatever rude line of questioning that Jeremy Paxman can lay on him.

The radio, as it tends to be, was more enlightening, with Joe Duffy's 'Soundbyte' leading on the Olivia bombshell. Now, the reasons were mostly professional, and only a bit personal. In ordinary language, it was a case of no hard feelings, but the show is a turkey, and I can't chase it around the block again in the autumn. Brendan O'Brien, who shared the sartorial tastes of his host during the Joe Dufflecoat era, and beyond, declared that he was going to call a spade a spade.

He venerated Olivia..."supreme professional"..."great journalist"..."feeling for the public nerve"..."enormous contribution"... and added that if Current Affairs isn't right, then RTE isn't right. He felt that the problem was a structural one, putting people of high ability and ambition into small boxes, and confusing the audience who identify with a distinctive flagship. Joe asked him whether Olivia was leaving Current Affairs at a high time or a low time, and Brendan plumped for "a medium time". This is calling a spade a gardening implement.

It suggests that things could be a lot worse. I fail to see how this can be, unless they run programmes on the type of furniture favoured by Ministers, whether they like eating out, or the condition of their golf handicap. 'Prime Time' was a miserable experience for all concerned. It had two states of being — bad and worse. It was bad when it had to deal with important stories in the kind of haste which suggests that the Gardai are banging on the door with a mind to book everyone for being "found on". It was worse when it began with dreaded words like, "But first, Bosnia."

It's not that I don't care about Bosnia, but with less than forty minutes a week to grapple with the agonies of Ireland, I don't care about Bosnia. The BBC does it much better, and we all have the BBC now. I believe that if there were forty hours a week of Current Affairs programming, down to the uninteresting adventures of Cavan County Council, there would still be an eager public lapping it up. Politics is the quintessential blood-sport in this country, and RTE television is depriving us of our kicks, leaving the radio people to sound almost demented with their zeal for jumping on a story and throttling it.

Life is infinitely more comfortable if you concentrate your energies on the Eurovision, displaying your toys to an indifferent world. RTE actually made a programme about making the Eurovision. I do not see the BBC making triumphalist documentaries which show how they didn't bugger up the British Open.

When the suits of Montrose turned yellow at the spectres of 'Scrap Saturday' and 'Nighthawks', it was clear that RTE had decided to be a politician-friendly zone, spiritually close to the Fianna Fail concept of RTE as a docile arm of the State. In suit-language, Current Affairs must be "balanced", "responsible", and "impartial", all of them synonyms for tedium.

Its ultimate thought-crime is that it is boring. We have a political culture teeming with low-lifes and grotesques and braggarts and shameless imbeciles, and RTE television contrives to render them boring. Defending this takes neck. Brendan O'Brien thought that it's "medium", and he's probably one of the smart ones.

Olivia's neck is finally at rest. She did the right thing. Her voice now carried conviction: It's Thursday, it's Prime Time, and it's not my fault.

They'll try anything once !

They are the ra-ra girls of RTE, and they are coming your way. The summer months bring them out in droves, though they work all the year round, roaming the countryside in search of good, clean fun.

There may be hundreds of them, or it may be just the one person, cloned from the cells of Anneka Rice. You know them to see, all right, but you can't quite put a name on them. What you know for sure is that if you win a prize of a car in a super competition, your all-purpose ra-ra girl will be the one who rings your doorbell and says "Mattie ? Mattie of the Nine Hostages ? You have won an Opel Astra and you're live on RTE television. What do you think of that ?"

They'd do anything for a laugh !

The crack squad of ra-ra girls really comes into its own on those RTE summer programmes which go right out there to meet the people where they live. The idea is that we've all had enough of that endless blather in grey Donnybrook studios, and it's about time to get a bit of fresh country air, to have a bit of a lark in rural Ireland.

Like the *Irish Times*' 'Summer Times' extravaganza, everything is bright and breezy and cheerful and optimistic and fun. Because you know what? It's official: people who live in the country do loads of interesting things! A typical adventure in the life of a ra-ra girl will go something like this: a woman will open the door of her house in a picturesque village, to be greeted by a ra-ra girl. "Oh, come on in," she will say, cleverly preserving the illusion by completely ignoring the RTE crew who are also her guests for the day. Then it's down to business, as the ra-ra girl reveals that this woman is the Line-Dancing Champion of Munster. Before you can say yee-haw, the ra-ra girl is dolled up in a howdy-hat and a cowgirl's outfit, and it's off to the Palais

De Dance for some serious *craic*. Ideally, she will round off the experience by sipping from a glass of Bud, winking at the viewers, and drawling, "So long, pardners!"

A ra-ra girl is one of the lads. She gives it a lash. Perhaps emboldened by all the cups of coffee she makes during the long nights after Samhain, she'll have a go at anything, from scuba-diving, to hay-making, to pottery. Since RTE's Ireland seems to have more potters per head of population than China has Chinamen, you'll find the ra-ra girl spinning the wheel like a trooper. It's always a great joke to play some funny music while the ra-ra girl makes a hames of her pottery. Then she will look eagerly to the taciturn master potter, who will assess her work with a kindly eye and say, "It's not bad for a first go. I'd say you show promise." Another day ends in bliss.

It is crucial for the ra-ra girls to make country people feel better about themselves, to boost their morale by indulging in their ancient customs and not doing it very well. The perfect scenario would involve an item about a ploughing champion. All the ingredients are in place here for ra- ra nirvana.

— "When did you start ploughing, Melchisedech?" — "Well, the father was good at the ploughing, so he showed me." Melchisedech will be a fiercely modest chap, shy in the face of his brash interlocutor, but somehow self-possessed, exuding mystical vibes. — "And do you think, Melchisedech, that a Dublin Jackeen like me would be any good at it ?" — "Sure, you can give it a go."

To a wacky soundtrack of galloping banjoes, she's off, opening up a furrow on the long acre, emitting the odd shriek as she presses the wrong button on the tractor, while red-haired children look on in bemusement. Then it is time to inspect the damage. — "It's harder than it looks, Melchisedech. Do you think I'll ever win the World Championship?" — "If you kept at it, I'd be getting worried."

Permanently breathless with wonder and enthusiasm for Ireland's rich tapestry, the one thing you will never hear the ra-ra girl saying is "Who would think...?"

Let me explain. Ra-ra girl is doing a piece to camera: "Here, in the idyllic little village of Ballyraddled, they are famous for amateur drama, for pottery shops, and for manufacturing hurleys. *Who would think* that behind this pretty facade lies a story that would make your hair stand on end, a story of human depravity that has made Ballyraddled the tranquiliser capital of Europe ?"

No, when the ra-ra girl comes out to frolic, the sun is always shining, the lambkins sport and play.

There are surprisingly few ra-ra boys in RTE, because they are too repressed to let themselves go. When the suits of Montrose bugger off for the summer to let the boys and girls make their mark, the boys dream of gravitas, of being Eamonn Lawlor for a day. They can't get too frisky, because they have their eye on the long dark nights after Samhain, when the suits are droning once more, and Ballyraddled is left to its own devices. It's hard to become a Regional Correspondent when you've been seen bungee-jumping on national television.

The boys hedge their bets, but the gals take the plunge. They just want to have fun, straddling the urban/rural divide.

You don't hear so much these days about the urban/rural divide. There was a time not so long ago when you heard of little else. It got a great old going-over in the mejia, the same urban/rural divide.

Every country in the world has people who live in towns and people who don't, but in Ireland, this arrangement caused a special divide. Perhaps this was due to the unusual conditions pertaining here, whereby we also have people living on other continents. Perhaps we just like being divisive.

As the 'Fair City' pay dispute raged on, it was worth reminding ourselves of the salient factors in the urban/rural divide. It came about through the realisation that people in rural Ireland have a superb quality of life, which is avidly sought out by people from less fortunate parts of the world, such as Germany. That they live in beautiful surroundings on large tracts of land, paying no tax, and receiving free money from Brussels, while the ravaged wretches of Dublin prowl around their dismal housing-estates and satanic high-rise slums, trying to score heroin to get them through another meaningless day.

Furthermore, that the political fixers of rural Ireland ensure that a ridiculously disproportionate number of factories are built in their back yards, while the dole-queues of Dublin stretch to infinity. That rural Ireland is festooned with super-highways while mothers-of-eight in Tallaght weep for want of a bus to arrive in their lifetimes; that rural Ireland has the finest pubs in the world, while the badlands of Dublin have appalling drinking-dens the size of Wembley Stadium, full of men with tattoos whose mates are robbing your house while you're out; and that young people in rural Ireland are going to University just when many of their inner-city counterparts are checking into Mountjoy for the first time, to learn their abysmal trade.

I think that covers a lot of it, though some rural readers may want to rub it in by pointing out a few things that I've missed about their fabulous lifestyles. If they have any complaint at all (and they so rarely complain, to give them their due) it is that they can't put together a Gaelic team because their sons have emigrated to make their first million, to raise hell all over North America, and to lose their religion.

The surprising thing about the urban/rural divide as demonstrated by the 'Fair City' fiasco, is that these gross inequalities now appear to be institutionalised by a state body. Bela and the mangy gurriers of 'Fair City' were not looking for a lot, they were just looking for the same as what Miley and Dinny are getting for traipsing around Glenroe, trying to pass the time before the pubs open.

They wanted parity of esteem, and they were being spurned by the power-elite of RTE, many of whom are vengeful culchies who place less value on Bela's constant quest for his "hole", than on sheep-worrying in Wickla. Here it's a case of four legs good, two legs bad.

It is clearly founded on brute prejudice, because it does not even make basic economic sense. 'Fair City' is on an upward curve, and I really must watch it one day, while 'Glenroe' is developing those unmistakable signs of liver fluke, rincosporium, mange-mites, hoose, sucking lice, warblers and all those other maladies to which farmers are prey. Or is it their cattle? I can never tell from the ads.

Being the rural soap, of course, 'Glenroe' must be kept in the style to which rural Ireland is accustomed, regardless. Meanwhile, the 'City' cries out once more in pain, unheard, unheeded, forgotten, doomed.

THE RIGHT STUFF

The writer Martin Amis described the job of interviewing as one which requires a certain level of ongoing schizophrenia. If you are an admirer of the subject, there will be a natural human inclination to strike up a good rapport. If you have approved of someone from afar, it can be a bit dispiriting to discover that he is a thoroughly nasty piece of work, who treats your questions as though they were the bleatings of an imbecile.

In many cases, then, you will want to like your interviewee. But a voice in your head will be whispering all the while that it would also be rather handy if this nice person were to have a full-scale nervous breakdown somewhere in the middle of your opening gambit, weeping uncontrollably, making horribly indiscreet confessions about embarrassing personal foibles, offering perhaps to engage you in perverse acts, and generally carrying on.

The interviewer is seized by an almost sexual exhilaration when the person on the other side of the tape-recorder starts losing it in a big way. I remember being rigid with excitement when the reggae singer Dennis Brown — *Money In Me Pocket But I Just Can't Get No Love* — started losing it. We were conducting the interview in Montrose, where he was waiting to record a promo performance. In response to a simple question about Rastafarianism, the dreadlocked sage started banging on about the need to kill all homosexuals, or "batty guys", and his belief that menstruating women should be banished from his presence — "When woman is seeing her blood, she cannot come among I and I," he said, using the Rasta patois.

"Dennis," I thought, "You are awful, but I like you". Shortly after his tirade against batty guys — "dem for dead. I kill dem" — a well-known RTE homosexual stuck his head around the door.

I was speechless. "There you are now, Dennis, you're in luck," I thought. The prospect of winding up the proceedings with a spot of killing was an appalling temptation. And I still don't know whether I did the right thing by keeping quiet. The readers were denied a human sacrifice on banal grounds of compassion.

What, I wonder, would Paddy O'Gorman have done ? I think that I was thrown by the exceptional nature of the revelations, whereas this kind of thing is par for the O'Gorman course. On RTE's 'Queueing For A Living', or 'Lifestyles of the Poor and Unknown', people tell Paddy things about themselves which make Dennis Brown's little outburst sound like cunning media manipulation.

Paddy has no great interest in anyone who takes home more than £50 a week, so unlike an interview with a well-known person, his subjects have very little to lose by revealing all. He meets them outside courthouses or labour exchanges, or other such places of public humiliation, and away they go, sometimes inviting him home to hear the full story, as though to say, "Stop me if this is less than completely depressing".

He once sorted out the issues facing "Norn Iron" by eschewing the babble of politicians, and taking his mobile confession box to where the punters live in subterranean hostility to Downing Street Declarations, Hume/Adams Initiatives, and other such sophistry. He spoke to the loyal sons and daughters of Belfast, the poor folks, whose testimonies made the notion of a "United Ireland" seem like a joke which would scarcely make the grade in a Lucky Bag.

Quarantined from the Catholic species, a man out on parole spoke of his frustrations at being forced to attend a Day Centre in order to be acquainted with Taigs, where they made him take saunas and do weights. There was mild praise for the Loyalist paramilitaries, whose punishment shootings are carried out from behind, and are thus less crippling than those of the Provos, who blast away from the front. There was talk of racketeering, and the women were especially articulate about the hopeless routine of violence, the cheapness of life.

There will be no peace in our time, it is all too far gone. This is what the bould Paddy teased out, and any other form of inter-racial negotiation must be ultimately regarded as just a lot of big dinners in agreeable surroundings.

Granted, the bright side of the road is anathema to O'Gorman as he trawls the dark end of the street in search of the authentic voice of human desolation. You will know that you have hit rock bottom if you see him approaching you with a view to getting it all off your chest. He'd hardly bother you if you looked like you had anything going for you.

Most of us don't have the stomach for this kind of thing. We troop off to interview pop singers or actors, dreaming that they will whip out a syringe and start jacking up heroin for our edification. But we know that we will have to work incredibly hard for such a show. For Paddy O'Gorman, it would be a doddle. One look at him, and the old smack would be pumping away like blazes. He can't be that lucky, so it must be a touch of magic, a streak of real genius.

IRELAND ON THREE MILLION POUNDS A DAY

MONEY FOR NOTHING & YOUR CHIPS FOR FREE

It was the Festive Season, after all, and Albert Reynolds' triumph at the Edinburgh Summit, bagging all of that EC cabbage, was like someone arriving during the last dregs of a hooley with another crate of Scotch, causing much rejuvenation of flagging spirits, renewed revelry, and general bucklepping.

Muttering something about getting it for half-nothing from a Spanish fellow, his crucial intervention banished the short-term memory of the assembled ravers. Earlier on, mourning a disastrous Election campaign, they had been playing with a voodoo doll fashioned in his unflattering image, convinced that this year's Party was going to be the last one of its type.

"We can't go on like this," they had blubbered, right up until whisky galore arrived from bonny Scotland, and suddenly they who could not go on, could indeed go on with a vengeance for further orders.

Fianna Fail is still the party Party, and they will be doing the political conga long after their more straight-laced opponents are tucked up in their beds, leafing through C J Haughey's "Spirit of the Nation" for comic relief. The booty was explained in layman's terms as constituting three million pounds a day. Hey, it's the Three Million Quid A Day Gang ! Let there be dancing in the streets, drinking in the saloons, and necking in the parlours.

The mood of the Party was transmogrified from one of self-flagellation, confusion, and depression, into a bracing sense of a new challenge, based on the idea that if three million quid a day is about to be doled out, it will be done with a Fianna Fail paw. It probably pans out at something like a pound for every man, woman and child, but a pound is a pound, and since it was Albert and his little helpers who brought it all back home, it is he who should play Santa Claus, ho, ho, ho.

Some people wondered if they could have their pound sent on in the post, missing out the middle-man, just in case we have to give it all back eventually.

It was once suggested that the reason Ireland has milked the EC more successfully than most, is that the paymasters are so brain-addled after ploughing through a 1,000-page Dutch Feasibility Study, or an equally massive Belgian Development Proposal, that when they are finally confronted by a beaming, garrulous Irish person, perhaps a little the worse for drink, pleading "Ah, go on lads, give us a few bob lads, ah go on lads," they just sign the cheque out of relief and exhaustion.

Three million quid a day. Ah yes, it has a seductive purr in these days when Fianna Fail are not only unsure who to go to bed with, they can hardly remember where they live any more. Perhaps they think that if they keep wandering around those Ring Roads, they will eventually find the old homestead, and hope to Christ that the key still fits.

Ring Roads, that great national growth industry. At the current rate of going, this country is going to look like Spaghetti Junction by the year 2,000, with everyone driving around to no apparent purpose like Raftery the Poet on wheels, listening to Gay Byrne telling them that the country is now more banjaxed than ever before, and laughing hysterically as they contemplate causing a massive motorway pile-up for a bit of diversion.

Infrastructure is the word, and we are fast becoming the Infrastructure Kings of Europe. Critics will argue that there is a supreme pointlessness in getting from A to B speedily and efficiently, if A and B have all the vibrant prosperity of the Dust Bowl on a particularly windy day. But hey, who gives a shit ?

The Euro windfall was in the grand old tradition of the Christmas Box from Amerikay, and a grand old traditional Party like Fianna Fail should be there when it's received, to share in the wonder of it all. As for "the Economy", whatever that is, it's a long road that has no turning. And we will know all about long roads in the difficult years ahead.

Then in keeping with tradition it began to go horribly, horribly, wrong. Dick Spring went to "Europe" again to give it another lash with Jacques. One can only imagine the warm feelings which welled up in the feisty Frenchman's breast as his favourite peripheral tribe once more engaged him in a bout of "negotiations".

According to RTE's Tommie Gorman, Delors' hands were trembling as he was introduced to some Irish journalists. The little fellow was obviously in a state of high anticipation as he readied himself for another session of Hibernian cut-and-thrust. There were also reports that Delors had taken to throwing tantrums out of the blue, suggesting that our negotiators should come with an EC Health Warning. We were expecting to hear rumblings from Brussels of how Delors has been seen in animated debate with rubber plants, that he has been weeping uncontrollably for no good reason, and that sources close to the Commission have described him as "a chronic bed-wetter".

It's those old communications problems again. It has been the great curse of Irish politicians in recent times, this failure to agree on what actually happened, or whether, in fact, it happened at all. Commissioner Bruce Millan was sure that he said £7.3 billion, Albert Reynolds was sure that Jacques Delors said £8 billion, Dick Spring heard £7.84 billion, or something that would become £7.84 billion when the light caught it a certain way.

At one stage, the figure of £8.7 billion was dancing around Mr Reynolds' head, like a ballroom owner who reckons that it always eventually pans out at £8.7 billion when the Joe Dolan takings are counted. Now, Dick Spring was hearing voices saying £7.84 billion again, after an intimate eyeball with the increasingly distracted Commission President. At one point, Monsieur Delors appeared to have dropped Bertie Ahern in the *merde*, but Bertie, magnanimous to a fault, forgave him.

Overall, we must conclude that either Jacques Delors is not very good at English, or our chaps are not very good at English. And indeed, much was made of Delors' lack of dexterity with the language, with our boys portraying him as a prime candidate for a starring role in 'Allo, Allo', if and when his current duties became too onerous. "I say no, and I am very worry against that, very worry, because this is a liar," he quipped good-naturedly to the merciless newshound Gorman.

So when Delors told them to go forth and build a rake of Ring-Roads, did he actually mean that they were to ring Roadstone and enquire about a rake? Will somebody please check this? Alternatively, it may be the case that when the Irish come to play, the common EC language becomes a strained form of Swahili, known only to a few mystics.

I have not been the only one to observe that all of this is politics as it might have been practised by the late Tommy Cooper. Pick a number...any number...say abracadabra...and fall flat on your backside. The Cooper analogy stretches to the fact that, like some of our Eurovisionaries, his public persona was that of a man who doesn't quite know why he was there, and whose tricks are likely to flop with hilarious consequences.

The eight billion quid that never was cast our representatives in the mould of the local Lothario who emerges from out of the night claiming that he "got the leg over" at the back of the hall, when he really only dribbled over his partner's shoulder while lurching around to 'Je T'aime'. In this light, the jeering opposition saw the Spring mission as a plea to the reluctant partner not to let the cat out of the bag, to save face with the lads.

And as our representatives strove to achieve a cosmic harmony known only to them, the rest of the world grumbled monotonously, "That is not what I meant at all. That is not it at all."

Monsieur Delors retired from public life to read good books.

The genius of the Reynolds administration for financial creativity continued with the announcement that the Taoiseach was "giving serious consideration to a plan to turn the entire Shannon basin into a giant tax-free zone". Holy shit.

The idea was that you would have a 180-mile long "corridor" extending the length of the Shannon for five miles on either side of the big river, within which tax incentives would encourage what was described as "a huge range of manufacturing and service industries". A huge range. Huge beyond the dreams of hugeness. In its ambition and originality, it smacked of The Return Of The Hot Money pantomime. This had been a fucking brilliant idea altogether, offering an amnesty to tax evaders if they agreed to cough up a small percentage of their hot money. Shades of *My Beautiful Laundrette*.

Comparing the "corridor" to the Urban Renewal Scheme, whereby inner-city areas of Dublin and Cork are refurbished, aided by tax allowances, a Reynolds supporter said that "The Shannon scheme would be far more wide-ranging and would affect virtually half the country". The principle of the thing seemed to be quite interesting. To counter the usual complaints about rich culchies paying no tax, it was surely fair to consider an extension of the scheme.

Why not extend the five-mile boundary to, say, forty miles, or even a hundred miles? A speculative figure like five miles is bound to cause a bit of grief somewhere along the line. And why should the Shannon alone be extended this largesse? What about the Lee, the Blackwater, the Slaney, the Boyne, the Barrow, the

Nore, the Suir, and the Garravogue itself? They too have their story, and are no doubt only dying to be inundated by "a huge range of manufacturing and service industries", whatever the fuck that is.

I detected something ancient and visceral about Mr Reynolds' generosity to the fellow with his head in the tax-man's noose. A broadly Christian view, which hated the sin, but loved the sinner. Perhaps his love was too great?

This, after all, is the man who saved the whale. Him and Noel Dempsey. The International Fund For Animal Welfare took out a full page ad in the *Irish Times*, heaping gratitude and adulation on the diffident shoulders of Mr Reynolds and his able deputy, the boy Noel.

At a meeting in Mexico, the International Whaling Commission voted to establish the Southern Ocean Whale Sanctuary, which will effectively protect ninety percent of the world's remaining whales. The eulogy continued: "The outcome of the vote was in doubt right up to the last minute, so those of us who care deeply about these majestic mammals turned to sympathetic statesmen including Albert Reynolds and Noel Dempsey, to help secure victory for the whales." The job was oxo, our trusty environmentalists came through, and were awarded a badge of honour in the *Irish Times*, "on behalf of the whales". All hail Albert, Prince of Whales!

If only we could see ourselves as others see us. In the urge to run ourselves down, we so often lose sight of the potential for greatness within us. What on earth gave these people the idea that Albert Reynolds is a statesman sympathetic to whales? Have we ever looked at Noel Dempsey and thought, "By the cut of his jib, that fellow will go to the wire for the majestic mammal?"

We have not.

As Flann O'Brien suggested, we are crippled by our false, self-serving perceptions of others. His wife, for example, thought that he was a husband, when in fact he was a philosopher.

With Albert Reynolds, we churlishly thought of words like "ballroom", "pet food", "crap" and "massive damages". Others think of words like "sympathetic statesman". With Noel Dempsey, we think of the Gang of Four and Mullaghmore. Others dub him "saviour".

So who is this "Albert Reynolds" about whom we clearly know so very little? He had apparently become Taoiseach for no good reason that you could think of other than to gallop around the world meeting boring businessmen and talking about factories. His ego seemed to diminish with the job in direct proportion to the way that his predecessor's ego appeared to swell on the strength of it.

There seemed to be little in it for him apart from hard knocks and dog's abuse and the fucking Beef Tribunal. His soul seemed unexcited by Big Ideas. Sure, he wanted "peace" in the North, but Mad Dog McGlinchey probably wanted "peace" as well, under certain strenuous conditions. Tell us something we don't know, Albert, we whined. Raise your gaze above the number-crunching banality of it all and offer us your vision of the cosmos.

There had been subtle hints of a burgeoning nobility in some of his Dail performances. Though he never altered his demeanour in the House from that which is commonplace in Longford County Council, in dodging the Opposition's harpoons, he started lambasting the vice of "playing politics". Lower than this a person can not stoop, he appeared to be saying, and how it grieved him to say it. "Playing politics" is an ugly business, and it saves no whales.

He and Dempsey did not play politics abroad in Mexico. There was no significant political capital to be made, no "passports for whales" angle. Granted, there was no political disadvantage to it either.

For all its many virtues, Longford is decidedly inland, and depriving a few Japanese degenerates of their blubber and their aphrodisiacal testicles was unlikely to have lasting repercussions on the crusade for that overall majority. It will be no excuse next time around to say that Fianna Fail blew it by buggering up that crucial Oriental vote in the marginals. And the party fixers have yet to devise a way of getting whales to vote one, two, three, Fianna Fail.

By a giant leap of the imagination, you could accuse Mr Reynolds of making a blind stab at Eoghan Harris' concept of the Moby Dick factor, that elusive floating vote waiting to be harpooned by those who pursue it with enough guile and intensity. But Albert was probably happy enough looking at the beached Moby Dick Spring for that.

If you want to crawl as low as a snake's belly and "play politics", you can argue that Reynolds' and Dempsey's love for endangered species did not extend with the same fervour to Mullaghmore, and absolutely not to the Progressive Democrats. They could save the whale, but they couldn't save a bit of oul' scenery in Clare. Physician, heal thyself.

Those of us who despise playing politics will discern an environmental instinct which was always central to Albert Reynolds, particularly in the area of recycling. He recycled pig's guts into dog food, he recycled his Fianna Fail opponents into political dog food, and his beloved show bands were world leaders in recycling a few chords into musical dog food.

Way back, he and a few like-minded individuals even recyled Charlie Haughey. And by sticking to "one sheet", his concern for forestry became a thing of legend.

Yet, when the old hippie cliché about saving the whale was doing the rounds, they never remotely envisaged that salvation was to come in the person of Albert Reynolds, rising like an avenging Neptune from the deep blue fathoms, with Noel Dempsey by his side, trident drawn.

So it goes and thar she blows.

Having saved the whale, Albert's fans and supporters were angered at the way that he was characterised by the popular comedian, Mr Dermot Morgan. During his performance at the National Entertainment Awards, RTE subscribers heard Mr Morgan refer to Mr Reynolds as a "Longford knacker". Fianna Fail heavy hitter Noel Davern described it as a cheap stunt, and suggested that RTE should look at the way that it is promoting Mr Morgan.

There were only two errors in this. The first error is that it was not a stunt, cheap or otherwise, it was just part of the act which is widely available on the Dermot Morgan Live video. And the second error is that RTE has, in fact, looked at the way it was promoting Mr Morgan. It did this a long time ago, and decided that it would promote Mr Morgan as little as possible.

I think that what we had here was a serious misunderstanding of both comedy and democracy. Political comedy or satire is at its most effective when it irritates the hell out of those that it satirises. And it is somewhat less than democratic for politicians to be encouraging the national broadcasting service to damage the livelihoods of people who get on their wick.

Morgan took the stand to state his defence: "The essence of the gag was contrasting Mr Haughey's imperious nature with Reynolds' 'everyman' approach. The idea that he might sell you a carpet from the back of his Jag. Like any caricature, you exaggerate things slightly. In contrast to the Napoleonic Haughey, here was a man who would "break up horses for dog food, or get your driveway re-gravelled for you."

Morgan might have added that a man who has dealt in the entrails of beasts would be familiar with the odd knacker's yard, but he rejected this sophistry: "It was just a bit of abuse. It's just ridicule. That's all it is. In Longford, they said that a man there nearly put his foot through the television set. I hope it was one of those ones up on a high shelf, that he tried a Bruce Lee and crucified himself. I mean, where do they get off with this shit? This preciousness?"

But there were jokes too, like the Fianna Failers who complained of insensitivity to travellers, a concern which is never far from their minds. That was a good one.

Before the Peace Process, and the Golden Age of Albert Reynolds, so tragically brief, there were times when you got the impression that our then Taoiseach was unhappy with us. This was a reversal of the normal relationship which applies in these matters, because, in all fairness, it is surely our prerogative to be displeased with the Taoiseach.

He would keep a low public visibility during certain times of crisis. This elusiveness reached its apogee on the day after the devaluation of the Punt, when it was learned that Mr Reynolds was enjoying a performance of *Miss Saigon* in the darkness of a West End theatre. Critics suspected something more than just advice from the National Fondlers, foolishly urging him to keep his gob shut no matter what. They sensed a vaguely peevish edge to his rare public pronouncements, like when he told the Dail that he had created more jobs than the whole lot of them put together. But sure, that's women for you.

Otherwise, he could seem merely aloof. He kept saying that he'd said things before, he was saying them now, and he would say them again. What exactly he had said before, was saying now, and would say again, tended to get lost in the heat of indignation. He was always muttering a few words about things being "on the table". This particular item of household furniture seemed to loom large in his vision of diplomacy. On a range of issues, everything was on the table — if you had a table — presumably including false teeth, wooden legs, and even toupees, if needs be.

Some saw a man sulking at the fickleness of his people, who initially welcomed him as "a businessman", a practical individual who would sweep away the grandiose posturings of Emperor Haughey, and who then rounded on him as the One Sheet Man, whose performance at the Beef Tribunal displayed all the statesmanlike attributes of a used car dealer. He was losing it in the Golf Club lounges, where they had reluctantly accepted him as the sort of fellow who wouldn't be sitting in his office late at night, thinking up ways of raising their taxes. You could take the man out of the Show Band, but you could not take the Show Band out of the man, they jeered.

Eventually, he was in the excruciating position of being one of the few politicians since records began who did badly out of a favourable opinion poll, implying that the less we saw of him, the more we liked him. Unfortunately, in politics, when absence makes the heart grow fonder, it is usually the prelude to separation proceedings.

By appearing to be thin-skinned, he had ignored a grim little pact which all Irish politicians must make with us, the unfortunate punters. He actually announced that he was not going to tolerate being excoriated on a purely personal level, apparently oblivious to the blatant reality that this is precisely the price we demand for letting many of our representatives loose in the corridors of power, at our expense.

Considering some of the characters we have elected over the years, they surely to God don't think that they are there for any reason other than a bit of cheap diversion? And in this fair deal, many of them have duly delivered, to their credit, and our grim satisfaction.

It is not that his tormentors cared too much if they never saw Mr Reynolds' increasingly care-worn visage from one end of the year to the other. Indeed, the truth was demonstrably to the contrary. The problem arose when they perceived that their man was in a bit of a funk, and as Brian Lenihan, one of the noblest Irish politicians in the traditional style, has pointed out, perceptions are important.

Mr Haughey, for example, could disappear for months at a time, but his invisibility was of a different nature, because we surmised that he was up to all manner of wonderful things, enjoying himself on our behalf. Even if we sensed that his approach to personal slights was one which involved the imaginary application of hurleys to the offenders' private parts, there was something almost healthy in this, a willingness to engage in the national blood-sport.

It was the curmudgeonly attitude which critics couldn't accept, since Taoisigh ought to be thoroughly delighted with themselves for emerging so well from the wreckage over which so many of them preside. They didn't want Mr Reynolds to pretend that he could do anything, indeed they clearly didn't want him to do anything at all, if he didn't feel like it. But it would be nice if he looked like he was enjoying not doing it.

Out of Ireland, he was having a great time. He went to Malaysia and "stressed the similarities" between Ireland and Malaysia. I suppose, no more than the Malaysians, we are doing our best to turn the few shillings in a hostile world, though with conspicuously less success than the lads beyond in Kuala Lumpur, where money is not an issue among the work force. Other similarities include the fact that we both belong to the same species, *homo sapiens*, with all that this entails. The need for food, water, and shelter, and the ability to walk upright, are obvious points of similarity here.

If he had stressed the differences between Ireland and Malaysia, he would still have been there to participate in the Millennium celebrations, but with the plane gathering dust on the runway, and the old urge to travel upon him again, it was up and away once more into the beckoning skies. Between himself and Mary Robinson, the rest of the world must think that we are a nation of chameleons, who would think nothing of arriving in Papua New Guinea, and extolling the ancient ties of friendship and co-operation between our indomitable peoples.

On his travels, he was "selling Ireland" for a price as yet to be agreed. He was also picking up a moxy-load of university degrees, and could justifiably have run down the aisle of the Government jet yelling "Let me through, I'm a Doctor!" He was conferred, *inter alia*, with an Honorary Doctorate of Law at New

York University. How, in the name of the Lord Jesus Christ and his Holy Mother they arrived at this decision is anyone's guess, though his amazing performance at the Beef Tribunal may have impressed New Yorkers in a way that is not readily visible to the native Irish. Yet the image of the One Sheet Man with his One Sheet Scroll is a curiously appropriate, even poignant one.

Another clue to the mysteries of academe is the fact that having been conferred at NYU, Dr Reynolds, resplendent in funny hat and gown, was due to lead a procession of the usual Irish award-winning types — Seamus Heaney, Cyril Cusack, James Galway, Brian Friel, Mary O'Hara etc. — with their Presidential Medals, through Washington Square. As it happens, Washington Square is one of the most notorious places in New York, its denizens consisting of a lurid assortment of crack dealers, pimps, winos, muggers, flashers, and low-lifes from many lands whose idea of social etiquette involves sidling up to innocent strangers and hissing, "Hey, Meester, how much you take for the old lady, hah?" And that's just the women.

What these grand old types made of Dr Reynolds with his newly acquired gravitas, leading this parade of shiny, happy Gaels through their territory, beggars the imagination. But for sure, there were enough laws being broken in the immediate vicinity to give the good Doctor, albeit one of five-minutes standing, ample material to keep his practice going well into the next century.

What the Doctoring of Albert Reynolds means for the status of third-level education is hard to tell in an American context, where you can acquire PhDs in everything from tarot-reading to turnip-snagging. You could probably get one in Ballroom Management, if you were of a mind to.

His supporters touted him as a potential recipient of the Nobel Peace Prize, but he was far too peaceful to be seriously in the running for that. Previous recipients include Sean McBride, a man not unfamiliar with the business end of a revolver, Menachim Begin, the pioneer of the car-bomb, and Henry

Kissinger, whose award must have caused heated controversy down Cambodia way.

Honorary Doctorates appear to be the Universities' way of thumbing their noses at the regular punters, whose poor mothers and fathers put them through college at great personal hardship, so they can learn how to roll a joint properly, or crack open a bottle of Smithwicks with their teeth, while the "honorary" crowd are off making their first million, having decided that book-learning is for the birds.

Mrs Robinson has been collecting them at a furious rate, but she was always a very brainy girl, and would probably have acquired a few under her own steam. Nonetheless, congratulations were in order to Dr Reynolds...I presume.

And when students come to reflect on the men who have been Taoiseach, there will be a special place for Albert Reynolds, and the innovations he brought to the style of government. His was the first Government-On-Tour, forever on the move from town to town. Advances in travel technology mean that you can gig in Dublin, Hong Kong, Sydney, Christchurch, and Honolulu in one flourish. And run the country while you are at it. Up there, where the air is clear, you can think about your plans to "de-humanise the Social Welfare system". You can think about Ireland on three million pounds a day, tired but happy.

From the Antipodes, he checked in for long enough to talk to the Tanaiste about some ugly business concerning the handing out of big jobs on the bench. A few minutes on Irish Steel, perhaps, a minute or two about Team Aer Lingus, and a lot of chawing about Harry Whelehan. They'd sort that out the next time he was in Ireland. They'd let a bit of light in on that one, eventually.

The Tanaiste then put his Tanaisting to one side and fetched up at the United Nations in New York. We now had no Tanaiste living and working on the island of Ireland. Charlie McCreevy was in Chicago, gigging with Bord Failte. Bertrand Ahern,

Chancellor of the Exchequer, was in Canada, talking big money. Ruari Quinn was in Brussels, at an EU meeting. Brian Cowen went along, too. And so did David Andrews. Noel Dempsey was in the Lebanon, entertaining the troops. And President Robinson was in Zambia, where Irish missionaries have gone before her.

The Taoiseach still set an inspirational tone by visiting Hawaii on his Grand Tour of the English-speaking Peoples. Why Hawaii? Because it is there.

There are few discernible links between Ireland and the land of Steve McGarret and his sidekick, "Book 'em" Dano. The odd fugitive IRA man has turned up there, working as a cocktail-shaker and living with his common law wife, Moon Flower, but the connections are extremely flimsy on the whole. What can be said for Hawaii is that it is a very nice place, with lovely weather and terrific beaches and mighty surfing, and where friendly women greet you at Honolulu Airport with a garland of exotic flowers. Elvis' *Blue Hawaii* is one of his best bad films, so there was a cultural flavour to the jaunt. If there is an Irish community in Hawaii (all hail the Hawaiian Irish) they will rustle up a bit of an oul' doctorate and warn you about the Curse of Lono.

Suitably refreshed, the Great Aviator then made a courtesy call to Ireland, to meet Boris Yeltsin at Shannon. God bless us and save us.

They couldn't have had much in common anyway, as Mr Reynolds doesn't drink. A bit of a downer after the paradise that was Honolulu. We have been told that we can't all live on one small island, and we should not expect the Government to live here either, if they can help it. Tabloid newspapers were carping about the Government-In-Exile, apparently ignorant of the wonders of global telecommunications. Michael Woods, dubbed the Home Alone Minister, assured the nation that Mr Reynolds would be told about an invasion. "We would not be going to war without the Taoiseach being informed," he told Marian Finucane.

This Virtual Leader, this remote-control Taoiseach, this Zoo Government, reminded critics of such statesmen as Ronald Reagan, who regarded the presidency of the United States as a part-time job. Reagan was fast asleep for a large proportion of his eight-year tenure, but then the Evil Empire fielded leaders who officiated at important State occasions while being clinically dead. Like Reagan, Reynolds had a tendency to contract foot-in-mouth disease, but Reagan still got the credit for winning the Cold War, just as Reynolds was feted from Ballinamuck to Brisbane as Peacemaker.

They both had an "aw shucks" attitude to the bamboozling minutiae of policy, coming across as regular guys who are only trying to do their best. Reagan was probably the original one-sheet man. From the Teflon President to the Teflon Taoiseach, these men had more in common than a background in show business.

This was the Taoiseach as multi-national mogul, the hands-off potentate keeping an eye on the store with phone calls from the belly of the great white bird, nipping nimbly through the nimbus, because it is there. He nearly clocked up more flying time than Yuri Gargarin, and for a while there, he was looking like the first Taoiseach to land on the Moon. In orbit around the planet which he had left in Peace, he could do no wrong. At that time he could have dashed off a memo ordering the slaughter of Progressive Democrat first-born, and received what Gerry Adams calls "a guarded welcome". The Beef Tribunal report would be buried under an avalanche of bullshit and Peace. Everyone would be "vindicated", even though they said so themselves, and every man would have forty acres and a mule.

Signs on it that when his feet finally touched the ground at Shannon, and Yeltsin wouldn't come out, Albert's fortunes began to go into kamikaze mode. Bad karma beckoned. The baleful gods were about to extract their price in full.

In fairness, Yeltsin is far from being the only member of his tribe who enjoys a glass of wine with a meal. When Boris' enemies holed up in the Russian White House, Mr Ruslan Khasbulatov, Chairman of the Parliament, was said to be looking "harried and weary". Wearing a bullet-proof vest under his suit, describing Yeltsin's government as "fascist", he vowed to fight to the end.

On RTE Radio, Orla Guerin expanded on his "harried and weary" condition by noting that he was "so drunk that he could barely speak". The Foreign Minister, Andrei Kozyev, further embellished the picture by saying, "A lot of people there are drunk. They are armed. Some of them are mentally disturbed."

Casting one's mind back to the last major power struggle in Moscow, one recalls the spokesperson for the anti-Gorbachev plotters, Comrade Yanayev, addressing the media in a tired and emotional manner, with his hands visibly trembling. Was this a result of the understandable stress he must have been enduring as a party to a cataclysmic political upheaval? In part, I suppose that it was.

Mainly, though, it was The Drink. He was boozed to the gills and feeling like a poisoned pup. Whenever two or three of Boris' compatriots are gathered to toast The Motherland, the idea begins to form, "Lads, let's get completely rat-arsed and take over Russia!"

There is a certain twisted logic to this phenomenon, in the sense that you would need to be totally out of your gourd to entertain the appalling prospect of running Russia. The downside is that vodka frenzy leads to a cavalier dismissal of such rudimentary elements of a successful coup as popular or military support. Comrade Khasbulatov did remember his flak-jacket, but he may have just slept in it.

On the morning after a glorious revolution, one can imagine a Russian plotter mumbling to his wife, "I am absolutely ripped to the tits, Olga. What did I do last night? What did I say?" — "Well actually, Yuri, you announced that you were taking over Russia". — "Boys, oh boys, I must have had quite a skinful. Still, no harm done, I suppose, no reporters around." — "Not quite, Yuri. You announced it on national television. You and Vladimir, and Oleg. You invaded the station during the 9 O'Clock News and declared that the old order is dead. The police are in the hall now. They say you'll be out in twenty-five years with good behaviour."

Yeltsin cuts a perplexing figure in all of this. It is widely accepted that Boris would drink the cross off an ass. A man of whom it was said, "For Boris Yeltsin, America is a bar five thousand miles long". It is his great misfortune that he contrived to be fairly sober on the odd day when it mattered, and was carried along by the irresistible momentum of events, which has resulted in him holding down one of the worst jobs in the world, when he could be having a great time getting mouldy drunk and being fished out of the Volga by his jolly comrades.

So many of these Russian pols look like serious boozers, not least his key opponent, Alexander Rutskoy, who, if I am any judge, would knock it back to a band playing. How absurd, then, in this dipsomaniacal setting, for Messrs Thatcher and Reagan to claim credit for the collapse of the Evil Empire. The reason why Mikhail Gorbachev cashed his chips has little to do with nonsense like the Cold War, or the lax introduction of market reforms. He went to the wall for one overwhelming reason: he quadrupled the price of vodka.

"Russia sober is Russia free," he seemed to be saying, though echoing another Irishman, he might have added, "This night, I have signed my death warrant." In the immortal words of journalist Bill Graham, the Soviet Union was like an entire continent being run by the GAA. You'd think that Boris would like it here.

Let's face it, any meeting between the leaders of Ireland and the Russian Bear is not going to be a meeting of equals. Those lads were sending chimpanzees into outer space before we had completed the Rural Electrification Scheme. We, in turn, used to pray like mad for their deliverance from Godless Communism, pitting our Rosaries against their rockets.

Boris gave us another spin on the high moral ground with his sleep-over at Shannon, but he invited Albert to Moscow to kiss and make up. He was no doubt alarmed to find that the Taoiseach who eventually visited him bore little resemblance to the man he left standing on the tarmac. I doubt if anyone bothered explaining the Fr Brendan Smyth Affair to him, or the strange case of Harry Whelehan. Albert Reynolds had either undergone massive plastic surgery, or Boris was more out-of-it than he had imagined.

"Never again" was indeed the sentiment all round, as world leaders came to Moscow to celebrate victory in the Second World War. For our brand new leader John Bruton, the sense of being somewhat less than equal must have been particularly acute on this occasion. A very sticky wicket. There is, to say the very least, something of a disparity between our official war efforts and those of the Russian Bear. We're talking 26 million dead versus The Glimmer-Man here. We're talking 26 million dead versus black bread and black market tay. We're talking 26 million dead versus a generation of children who grew up not knowing what a banana looked like, until the banana-boats came in again after the Emergency, and all was well again.

We're talking 26 million dead versus the FCA putting out tar-barrels in fields. We're talking 26 million dead versus taking captured German airmen out to the pictures. Ireland, the only country that prisoners-of-war didn't want to leave. We're talking 26 million dead versus wet turf.

Against all this, the Russian Bear being the sort of creature it is, we were still given a spin on the high moral ground, when the Taoiseach joined with other Western leaders in staying away from a military parade to a new war memorial, due to differences over the Chechen conflict. It seemed a bit churlish, all the same, when you consider that they put a halt to Hitler's gallop, while we galloped to offer our official condolences — to the Germans. They've earned their drink.

The best day ever he was, it would have been some job explaining to Boris Yeltsin why John Bruton arrived instead of Albert Reynolds.

Let us go now to a public house somewhere in Ireland. It is Christmas Eve, and Paddy is home from Australia, eager to discover just what the hell has been happening. He saw Albert Reynolds on the television in Sydney, and got a terrible fright. He and his brother Joe have both consumed approximately seven pints of ale. The hour is late.

PADDY: What's it all about then, little brother?

JOE: Well, there's this crowd called the Norbertines.

PADDY: Right. They're a Gaelic team somewhere up in Louth. You see, I haven't lost it. Good luck, good luck, good luck.

JOE: No, they're a religious order no-one had ever heard of before this Fr Brendan Smyth was had up on loads of sex abuse charges, the fucker.

PADDY: There's a lot of it about over in Oz as well. So how does this make John Bruton Taoiseach?

JOE: Well, the Attorney General, Harry Whelehan, didn't extradite Smyth for seven months, although he's not really supposed to extradite people. And the Cardinal was supposed to have put in a word for Smyth, but actually, he didn't. So people thought that the Attorney General should resign.

PADDY: Yeah, he had to go. Good luck, good luck, good luck.

JOE: But he didn't resign. What I mean is, he resigned, but he resigned as President of the High Court, It's all about the Beef Tribunal, really.

PADDY: Sex abuse at the Beef Tribunal?

JOE: No, not quite. Albert Reynolds wanted to make Whelehan President of the High Court because Harry did a good job on the Beef. They found out eventually that it was all the fault of the television reporter. But Albert promoted Harry when Dick Spring was out having a leak.

PADDY: So Dick Spring resigned.

JOE: No. Well, he resigned, as such. But only when they found out about more cases of sex abuse, and the Cabinet misled the Dail. That is, Finna Fail misled the Dail.

PADDY: Lying through their teeth.

JOE: Not exactly. They were misleading Dick Spring and misleading themselves as well.

PADDY: So they didn't mislead the Dail.

JOE: They did and they didn't. They want people to think that they're stupid. By the way, Whelehan never knew anything about it either. He was out shooting pheasants.

PADDY: So why did Albert Reynolds resign?

JOE: Fucked if he knows.

PADDY: Fucked if I know either.

JOE: Well, it's about trust, really. The new Attorney General, Eoghan Fitzsimons, threw the cat among the pigeons. Found a bit of paper lying around that explained everything. That's the one that the Cardinal didn't write. So he was sent to ask the old Attorney General to resign.

PADDY: So you have two Attorneys General?

JOE: No, just the one. Name of Dermot Gleason, from the Beef Tribunal. But you had two Taoisigh, Albert and Bertie Ahern. Except Albert was Acting Taoiseach, and Bertie never became Taoiseach. And Maire Geoghagan-Quinn piped up at the last minute to make a liar out of Dick

	Spring. Mind you, she tried to make a liar out of herself as well.
PADDY:	Sounds fair enough.
JOE:	It was all down to a journalist called Geraldine Kennedy.
PADDY:	It's all back to the Beef Tribunal.
JOE:	No, that was Susan O'Keeffe. Kennedy was the woman that was bugged by Sean Doherty.
PADDY:	Name rings a bell.
JOE	He made a speech about family values when Reynolds resigned. He said that Reynolds had a lot of family values.
PADDY:	He'll need them mate. So Dick Spring gets together with John Bruton and the Commie guy who looks like Georgie Best?
JOE:	Not quite. You see, Spring couldn't do business with Bruton. They don't like one another. Or at least they didn't up to last week. They like one another now. Anyway, Bruton couldn't be Taoiseach, he has no charisma.
PADDY:	And what about Georgie Best?
JOE:	Charisma. He's the leader of the Democratic Left.
PADDY:	What's the Democratic Left?
JOE:	Used to be the Workers Party, used to be Sinn Fein The Workers Party, used to be the Official IRA. They were great men for going to North Korea and raising a toast to the Beloved Leader Kim Il Sung on behalf of the risen people of Ireland. And they printed their own money.
PADDY:	So the blueshirts couldn't do business with them, unless to put them behind bars.
JOE:	No. Well, yes. They couldn't do business with one another, but now they can. They like one

another now. And Dick Spring likes both of them for the present.

PADDY: And that's how John Bruton became Taoiseach?

JOE: No. That's how Proinsias De Rossa became President of the United States.

THE OVERALL SMELL OF BRUTON

Sometimes I think that Albert Reynolds is still Taoiseach, but then, for the first six months of Albert's reign, I used to think that Charlie Haughey was still Taoiseach. It takes a while to adjust to a new regime, particularly so in the case of John Bruton, who assumed the position despite his best efforts. Like a dose of the flu, it takes a while to flush a Taoiseach out of your system, and to flush the next one in. Bruton only established himself in my mind as Taoiseach when he told a radio reporter in Cork that he is sick and tired of talking about the fucking peace process.

Albert Reynolds will never get sick of answering questions about the fucking peace process, you can be sure. He will answer them morning, noon, and night, in all conceivable circumstances. It is his baby, and he is devoted to it. He changes its nappy and sings it to sleep, and gets up in the middle of the night just to gaze in wonder at its peacefulness.

For Bruton, otherwise known as John Unionist, the bonding process was more difficult. He is growing to love it, but it is a contrary child, and its demands can get on his nerves after a long, hard day, running the country. Regardless, his ejaculation coloured in a missing element in the public's perception of its leader. Swearing, on or off the record, is fast becoming a mandatory activity for the leaders of nations, and Bruton had now made this essential break-through in a grand tradition which encompasses men such as Charles Haughey, John Major, Jacques Chirac, Boris Yeltsin, and any Australian Prime Minister you care to mention.

It is principally the fault of their media handlers that Taoisigh the world over cause such a flap when they talk dirty. Their utterances are so contrived and controlled, and their language is so constipated as a rule, that a spot of effing and blinding is the one sure way to gauge the authenticity of their remarks. There is still some doubt, even in the minds of the participants, as to whether Haughey thought that his fanfare of fucks in that *Hot Press* interview was on or off the record. But like John Major and the bastards who surround him, it didn't do Haughey any harm, and probably did him a lot of good.

There was Haughey at Fairyhouse, celebrating his Grand National triumph with John Bruton, a symbolic transfer of raw power from one fucking generation to the next. Welcome to the business, John, it's been a long time.

Jacques Chirac spoke the mind of his people when he told Margaret Thatcher at an EC Summit that she was talking bollocks. He is now the President of France. Boris Yeltsin is still staggering along, foul-mouthed drunk or sober, and Australia's Paul Keating would hardly have succeeded Bob Hawke if his people could not rely on him to match Hawke in feats of swearing. When Australian politicians dub one another "wankers", as they are wont to do, the people praise the clarity of their perceptions.

Back in the days when political reporters were more discreet about their leaders' displays of emotion, it was considered indelicate to inform the public that a Lyndon Johnson rarely completed a sentence without cussing, or that a Richard Nixon was given to pronouncements like "I don't give a fuck about the lira." Both men might have enjoyed a longer stretch in the Oval Office if reporters had been less prissy, and the plain folks had been exposed to the full blast of their vulgarity.

For John Bruton, the experience of high office has been particularly plagued by verbal and gestural constipation. He has been minded to a fault, and is said to be under instructions not to laugh out loud unless the urge is absolutely uncontrollable. Throw in the tortuous nuances of the peace process, where every syllable is subjected to forensic examination, and you can understand why he would need to let off a bit of steam, to loosen his trousers and let rip in the general direction of yet another journalist trying to pick his teeming brain.

Some commentators expressed alarm that Bruton could conceive for a moment of a world beyond the fucking peace process, even if there is more violence on the streets of Cork these days than in the boreens of South Armagh. They thought that it betrayed a certain detachment from this over-riding priority, and pined for a Reynolds-like passion, for fear that the Brits would start to play silly buggers. The Taoiseach talking about the fucking peace process is a bit like a Bishop giving out about the fucking Pope. It is a Bad Thought, an occasion of sin.

These critics say that the mechanics of the peace process are inherently boring, but that all parties must learn to love the boredom, to rejoice in its frugal comforts, and that journalists, too, have a responsibility to move the boredom forward in the higher national interest. Who would have thought that John Bruton, Mr Boredom himself, would cry out for a bit of diversion? Fucking no-one, that's who.

What is John Bruton doing being Taoiseach anyway, still leading Fine Gael, the Party which gave the world the constitutional crusade, the Tallaght strategy, and the Just Society.

Not.

When half the Party was desperate to get rid of him, and the other half was pretty keen, it looked like little more than a sad publicity stunt by a bunch of losers. For a few, brief, shining moments, they were centre stage, hogging the television cameras and the column inches, causing men and women who never did anyone a bad turn in their lives to hang around Leinster House in arctic conditions for about eight hours, waiting to take their photograph or record a statement. To make it worth their while, the mejia responded with imagery which was remarkably colourful in the context of an organisation which is normally painted in shades of grey, and which can be plunged into anarchy by the mere addition of a Twink.

John Bruton himself fired the first wild shot by saying that politics is not about presenting yourself like Rhett Butler. This was an unfortunate analogy in the circumstances, seeing as how Rhett Butler starred in a memorial to a way of life which has gone with the wind. The Mitchell boys, Jim and Gay, who, as far as we know are not related to Margaret, author of the Butler epic, dramatised the conflict by being filmed together, arguing on different sides of the motion. Here we saw the tragedy of it all, brother turning against brother, the saddest part of any Civil War.

If you failed to see the tragedy, you could certainly see the comedy in this, on the grounds that the battle for Fine Gael is not quite on a par with liberating the slaves of the Deep South. The Mitchell dilemma highlighted what looked like a cunning plan. With the end of Civil War politics, Fine Gael found that they had nowhere to go, so they thought that the best option was to stage their own Civil War. Internecine strife is bad for the nerves, but it is a great man for putting bums on seats, and that was Fine Gael's biggest priority at this juncture.

They did rather well out of their last serious schism, when Liam Cosgrave's condemnation of the mongrel foxes became the preamble to the era of Gentleman Garret Fitzgerald, and a period of Fine Gael affluence which now seemed as distant as the halcyon days of Tara. This time around, the Civil War was likely to be a bit too civil, as the issue was not one of ideology, but of personality, with the dissidents making the comical allegation that John Bruton is too boring to lead Fine Gael, whose past leaders, of course, were such wild and crazy guys, up for anything.

It was never going to have the raw, twisted passion of a Fianna Fail heave, with bus-loads of wild-eyed zealots arriving at Party headquarters to stage a chilling night rally. So the mejia had to oblige with as much excitement as they could muster, to run with the ball which Fine Gael had thrown to them. On 'Today At Five', Myles Dungan made a vague analogy between the fate of Bruton and that of Parnell. This was gilding the lily somewhat, since Parnell cashed his chips for being too interesting, whereas Bruton was facing charges of being too uninteresting.

The 'Six One News' was reduced to showing scenes of Alan Shatter leaving the meeting to get a few bottles of Lucozade, replacing the Party's lost energy but failing to replace its lost leader. There was the dramatic mercy dash of Senator Tom Neville, who jetted back from Namibia in an exhausted condition, prompting the obvious question of what in the name of jaysus was he doing out in Namibia in the first place.

Fine Gael can be grateful for the fact that the mejia abhors a vacuum, and that even if they failed to oblige with apocalyptic scenes in the style of Fianna Fail, they would still get plenty of mileage out of a little confusion. Even the deflationary emergence of Bruton, who chose this moment to make one of his dullest TV appearances of all, led to a newspaper headline, NOW FOR THE PURGE.

The full headline would have read, NOW FOR THE PURGE—WE HOPE, but instead, the humble survivor was muttering about policies, about education and the family and other such conversation-killers. If reporters are to endanger their health and sanity by freezing half-to-death taking pictures of Alan Shatter with bottles of Lucozade, they are entitled to a purge, to a few skulls mounted on sticks. Bruton would have to bathe himself in the blood of his enemies, and taste that intoxicating wine which would renew the Party's vigour.

Hoors for a bit of publicity, the Blueshirts then staged another coup, packing the 'Questions & Answers' audience with people who wished to state on national television that in the wake of the leadership contest, everyone should now get behind John Bruton.

It was as if all of the Old Reliables of the Q & A audience had been zonked on their way into the studio, their pockets rifled, and the precious tickets grabbed by young Fine Gaelers, old Fine Gaelers, and whatever remnants of Cumann na Gaedhal remain extant. It was such an impressive display of bucolic solidarity, that Ivan Yates appeared just a trifle embarrassed at one stage, something which I did not believe possible for a man in his position. The Old Reliables were well and truly cleaned out. There was no sign at all of the guy with the Tony Gregory aura, a Social Science degree from UCD, and a burning sense of rancour about all issues pertaining to the national condition. Gone, too, was his rancourous old uncle, the Behanesque character who is a concerned parent against drugs being sold by the wrong people, and who still seeks clarification on everything from the Downing Street Declaration to the result of the Grand National, and the time of day, if he is in particularly rancourous fettle.

You can see them coming a mile away, but then there is the subtle type, who begins his spake like a fairly normal person, until some telling turn of phrase, the use of the word "radical", or even some facial tic, gives the game away. Pee Dee alert ! Pee Dee alert ! Yet on this night, he slept with the political fishes, as did the sincere young person who calls for the views of other young people to be considered, but can't resist rounding off his spiel with the line, "as Dick Spring so rightly pointed out".

The environmentalist, the *Guardian* woman and the nutter from SPUC were also given a night off, their places usurped by girls who wear jumpers over their blouses, and who think that Ivan Yates really talks a lot of sense. I also missed the guy with the slightly bloated demeanour, who loses his train of thought, causing palpitations for John Bowman, who doesn't want to say "we've got a right one here", but who has a show to keep on the road. Somehow, this character pulls it out of the fire at the last moment, and we realise that it was just the authentic voice of Fianna Fail, straining to be heard.

All of these hardy perennials were eclipsed, and for one night only, the air was filled with the overall smell of Bruton.

Is he not fragrant?

ADVENTURES ON THE HIGH MORAL GROUND

Many moons ago, I saw John Bruton in Burgerland of Baggot Street, wolfing down a burger'n'fries before marching back up the road to run the country. Burgerland of Baggot Street is no longer with us, but John Bruton keeps rolling along, impervious to the tides of time or fashion. It was in some ways a poignant image, this plain man sustaining himself with a plain burger, his head full of weighty matters concerning the gross national product or the need for Dail reform. He mustn't have had time for the full meat tea.

Still hard at it many moons later, he failed to prosper in the opinion polls after Albert Reynolds cashed his chips. If he couldn't get a substantially improved rating after these shenanigans, it looked as though his only hope of impressing the punters in a big way was to bring the Olympic Games to Nobber, enter the 1,500 metres himself, and to win it in world record time. But Bruton would not be entered in one of the glamourous events. He would be in the 50 kilometre walk or some such grim contest which requires persistence and determination and stamina, worthy qualities which do not set the imagination ablaze.

Any verdict on Bruton was conditional on the enigmatic state of Fine Gael itself. When they plummeted to eighteen percent in the polls, it was hailed as a catastrophic embarrassment for which John Bruton had to be shafted. An alternative view was that they were doing remarkably well for a Party which hasn't had a big new idea since 1965 or thereabouts.

Perhaps he was playing a blinder and is their main selling point. There is always that possibility. I suppose he has been there for so long that he seems to have taken root in the Chamber. His turn would have to come, like the good Clongowes lad that he is. He could work up a great head of steam about the procedures of the House being violated, and be absolutely indignant about disrespect towards our sacred institutions, when the moment was crying out for a floor-show, a touch of Fred Astaire rather than Fred Flintstone.

That promiscuous liberal voter is not exactly enthused by the Brutonic aura, as he chooses to be interviewed in his office against a backdrop of enormous green tomes which might well be Law Reports, and which you suspect the man of actually reading for pleasure. He can come across as a parody of the self-image of Fine Gael Man. Responsible, respectable, reliable, upstanding, not the kind of chap who might have a rush of blood and wager the national debt on the outcome of the Galway Plate. Fine Gael Man stands aloof from brown paper bags full of used banknotes, though the bag-men of Fianna Fail will claim that it's just a matter of superior accounting procedures.

Ah yes, Fianna Fail. Whatever happened to them?

"Now is the time to join Fianna Fail," the advertisement said, alongside a photograph of a rather bronzed-looking Bertie Ahern. "Whatever your interests, your way of life, your ideals for the future, there is a place for you in Fianna Fail" it went on, casting a wide net across the nation's youth.

A bit too wide, perhaps? What if my interests are snuff movies and burglary, my way of life is entirely nocturnal, and my ideals for the future tend towards the imposition of martial law on Balbriggan? Is there still a place for me in Fianna Fail? Apparently so.

The Grand Old Party does need to assert its identity in these times of Coalition languor, to hold out the promise that Ireland will be free again some day, to keep their peckers up for the trials ahead. There is undoubtedly something of a lacuna in Irish public life at the moment, and Fianna Fail just happen to be at the wrong end of it at present. But in the nature of these things, as the political pattern becomes all too clear, their turn must come again. Theirs and everyone else's.

At the Fianna Fail end of the lacuna, they must somehow offer trenchant opposition to a government which is implementing and developing policies pursued by...er...Fianna Fail. There was a time when they could oppose anything that suited them, and then dismiss is all as harmless bullshit when Ireland was free once more. Now, as virtually all parties believe that they could form partnerships with everyone from Fine Gael to the Natural Law Party, Fianna Fail will continue to tweak a hamstring every time they make a charge across the floor of the House. They can point to a "difference of emphasis", to a distinctive nuance here and there, but a Fianna Fail Party which looks to nuance as its weapon of war, is as a eunuch on a wedding night, an untipped spear.

They laughed at Alan Dukes, but to a significant degree, they are all Tallaght Strategists now, whether they like it or not. The PDs are laying claim to certain leafy postal districts, as though they had never sat in Governments which plundered the taxpayers' pockets, and neutered enterprise. But they did, they did. And they will, they will. They want less Government, as long as they are members of it.

Really, what they all want is less government which happens to exclude them. With barely a ha'porth of difference between the squabbling factions, "transparency", and "accountability" have become the key factors in deciding who gets the next ride on the merry-go-round. If the man catches you acting the maggot, you are off.

In the world of transparency, there is also a difference of nuance, with Fianna Fail being perceived as having their paws in the till, while Fine Gael are more likely to be eyeing up the cash-register, flexing their fingers, tempted by natural greed, but limited by a sheltered upbringing. The PDs are sure that they could run the shop on more professional lines, while Labour, of course, are behind the counter, keeping a malignant eye on the lot of them.

It is all so unnecessary.

You would think that as a basic rule of thumb, a fundamental imperative on a par with putting on their trousers before venturing outdoors, politicians would beware the high moral ground. Dogs can be trained to avoid all sorts of things that are bad for them, but politicians will insist on flirting with the high moral ground, even though they have a gut instinct that this is akin to a naked man running blindfolded through a sawmill.

In their broad democratic vision, Fianna Fail recognise that ignorant people and morally indifferent people have a right to be represented too, and to hell with this niche-marketing shite. Though not exactly morally depraved, their sacred aspirations, like a United Ireland or the restoration of the Irish language, are such obvious comic fantasies, that only a fool would hold them to it. They have the common sense to set low standards, so that their stock rises through the mere absence of graft. They take twisted pleasure in the moral leprosy ascribed to them by the opposition, and laugh uproariously when Des O'Malley or Dick Spring develop their own ailments, and join the colony.

Spring, like O'Malley, made his leap for the high moral ground on the back of "the evil spirit", Charles J Haughey, and to a lesser extent on the back of Albert Reynolds' alleged relationship with the cattle-barons.

With ruffled nobility, Labour claimed they would do us all a favour by "keeping an eye" on Fianna Fail across the Cabinet table. Duly elected, they started flinging big jobs and perks at their relatives and associates, just acting normal, really, and tumbling down from the high moral ground to be confronted by the happy, smiling, faces of Fianna Fail, saying "Welcome to Hell, we were expecting you."

Down there, the Ethics in Government Bill, or the Keeping An Eye On Fianna Fail Bill, was bound to be a busted flush. As the passports-for-sale scandal unfolded, Michael McDowell went on a solo run, the last Pee Dee playing on the high moral ground, just like old times. He coursed Minister Michael Smith through the Dail and on the airwaves, and instinctively, the Fianna Fail hare responded to the notion of the prime Dublin Four hound tormenting the furry creature from the wild.

He pressed the atavistic buttons one by one, emoting about job prospects in the Midlands which an over-privileged Gonzaga smart-ass like McDowell just wouldn't understand. He resurrected Haughey's laceration of McDowell as one of the nastiest pieces of work to enter the House for a long time, and spoke with mock pity of McDowell's party, which will remain small for as long as it pursues such an unpatriotic line.

He implied that by chasing away decent Palestinians who only wanted to help Longford, and turn the few shillings for everyone, McDowell was motivated less by a zeal for ethics than by a congenital dislike of bogmen. Perhaps the highlight of these maunderings was the accusation that McDowell was "playing politics", this said with a perfectly straight face by members of the Fianna Fail party.

They were both playing politics, except that Fianna Fail were playing it as it lays, up to their necks in manure and still full of fighting talk, being "pragmatic", which means that if you can't be good, be careful, and if you can't be careful, make sure you don't sign anything. McDowell was in a much lonelier place, the high moral ground, and experience has taught us that this is probably the most dangerous place of all, a strictly temporary arrangement that is bound to end in tears. There is no passport that will get you down from there unharmed. It's the same for everyone. On the high moral ground, the brown paper bag is obsolete.

What is it with brown paper bags? In themselves, they are almost the definition of banality, functional for the most routine chores like carrying bottles of stout home from the pub, with perhaps some curry pie as a companion dish. Substitute money for stout and you are immediately into another realm of consciousness. To mention money and brown paper bags in the same sentence is to evoke a Pandora's Box of shady individuals and dark deeds. It may be a cliché, but there are frequent allegations that "developers" or their agents have bribed County Councilors with "money in brown paper bags", if they could see their way to fucking up the landscape a bit more.

I don't know why there is something reassuring about this wretched behaviour, but a wintry smile undoubtedly plays on my lips when I read about it. In a world of computer fraud and labyrinthine bank accounts stretching from Lyrecrompane to Liechtenstein, to places which are virtually a figment of the imagination, there is a pleasingly primitive ring to the notion of a wedge of crumpled notes in a brown paper bag. How quaint it all sounds in these days when political parties have organised the paying of tribute on more sophisticated lines. We were given to understand that donations to assist the democratic process were now conducted in cheque form, courtesy of meat moguls and the like, and overseen by debonair men sipping Perrier in agreeable hotel suites, with a German sports car parked out back. Fianna Fail may have been paper bagmen in the 60s, but in the 70s, they upgraded their "fundraising" ambiance to places like the Burlington Hotel, and now the "Burlo" is hardly good enough for them or the concerned democrats who wish to show their appreciation.

It is a theoretical proposition, but I wonder if there was ever any real need for developers to grease the palms of Fianna Failers or Fine Gaelers? Many County Councilors think that the environment is basically a nancy-boy preoccupation anyway, whereas for serious people, "areas of outstanding natural beauty" are literally for the birds. They grew up surrounded by all the outstanding natural beauty they could stomach, and nothing else, and they are sick of it. If pushed, they would quite seriously see little harm in building grand wee bungalows overlooking the Cliffs of Moher, and if it made the aesthetes want to throw up, there were enough paper bags going around to minimise the mess.

It is this bracing sensibility which would encourage developers to favour Councilors with their largesse, to keep more squeamish souls at a remove from the democratic mainstream. In the case of Dublin County Council, one-on-one brown paper bag rendezvous' are perhaps just a case of getting things done for sure, for sure. They are almost a romantic gesture, a token of long-standing appreciation, just a call to say "I love you", like Stevie Wonder.

Old-fashioned graft of this kind, the really crude stuff, lives on in a comical form with the Senate election process, perhaps because the Senate itself only lives on in a comical form. Here, a realistic candidate will bestow a range of attractive gifts on Councilors, because a failure to comply with the accepted convention would indicate both a lack of respect and a crippling naivete. I am reliably informed that one oft-returned Senator would fill the boot of his car with bottles of poitin for the Councilors, and boxes of chocolate for their wives. I suppose that in the unlikely event of the Councillor being female, some chocolate liquors would see you alright on the night. I am also reliably informed that the poitin would be camouflaged with innocuous wrapping of a kind that is as much a part of what we are as hare-coursing or emigration. I need hardly tell you that it was the brown paper bag, symbol of power, shield of our democracy.

We somehow expect these extremely busy people to deal with the profound moral issues of our time, such as the de-criminalisation of homosexuality. Doing my bit, I worked for some time on a form of words which might prove acceptable to those members of the Oireachtas who were wrestling with their consciences on this issue.

"In flagrant defiance of the views of the vast majority of decent people, and in deference to the opinion of a Court of so-called Human Rights who see fit to interfere in matters of which they know nought, it is hereby decreed that poofters be allowed to flaunt their perversions in full view of a scandalised nation, and there is nothing that we can do about it except weep for Mother Ireland."

Gerard "Gerry" Collins expressed it thus: "But for the fact that we have been brought to book by the European Court of Human Rights, we would probably not be giving it the priority that it is now about to receive....I believe that Europe is twisting my arm," he said. And we can't have Europe twisting Gerard Collins' arm. "Whether we should or we shouldn't, we're doing it," he said, neatly echoing the homosexual point of view, as well as a fundamental core value of the Fianna Fail Party.

On RTE's 'The Sunday Show', the tag team of Alice Glenn and Jim Tunney applied their capacious minds to the subject. "I personally don't feel that people who are so inclined suffer any great problems," said Tunney, the Yellow Rose of Finglas who was the best-dressed man in Leinster House. "It's a secret which has defeated humankind since humankind first existed," he reasoned. "If you have it, you have it," he said, as though he were talking about mastitis or ringworm. He did not think that society would be improved by "popularising" it, in the way, I suppose, that television popularised snooker.

Alice Glenn, drawing on her store of learning, appeared to disagree with Jim Tunney on the question of "having it". She thinks that you get it. "It's not a congenital condition. It is something that is acquired. It is generated through social contacts," she explained. So that's that then.

Of course, we never really enforced the laws on homosexuality, because to do so would have made us look like total fucking eejits. There are a lot of laws that we don't enforce because to do so would make us look like total fucking eejits, but there are sections of the community who like to have them on the statute books or in the Constitution anyway, just for pig-iron. There they stand, these pious aspirations, wondering if someone will be silly enough to enforce them. The Constitution is a bit like "the economy", a set of theoretical propositions which keep the zealots amused, but which seem to belong to a parallel universe, uninhabited by humankind.

We used to be a bit more literal-minded about such things.

When Tomas MacGiolla became Lord Mayor of Dublin, he was the first incumbent of the Mansion House to have been imprisoned for his beliefs. It is surely safe to say that he will be the last. If any of his successors from the up-and-coming generation of politicians happen to wind up in the chokey, it will certainly not be for their beliefs. To intern a modern Irish politician for his or her beliefs would be like accusing Anna McGoldrick of being ineffectual in the Middle East peace process. They would be totally innocent as charged.

De Valera's method of dealing with subversives would nowadays be regarded as a trifle draconian and anti-social, but it may not be wholly without merit. I have heard it said, for example, that members of Ogra Fianna Fail and Young Fine Gael ought to be locked up. The reasons are never entirely clear, but have to do with a nebulous feeling that some kind of dramatic life-change would have to occur in order to free their minds of certain delusions. Selective internment would be controversial and costly, but I wonder if, perhaps, a spell in the army would be entirely wasted on them?

In fact, when I think of all the public representatives who might benefit from a spot of square-bashing, spud-peeling, boot-polishing and turkey-strangling, a vision begins to form in my mind of Ireland ascending to the status of a military superpower rivalled only by the United States.

For Tomas MacGiolla, being interned in the Curragh from 1957 to 1959 was not an entirely negative experience. For a start, he became Tomas Mac Giolla for sure, finally abandoning the pretence of being Tom Gill. He could bone up on his Irish in the long nights after Samhain, and this is no bad thing. So, too, could Frank Ross, later Proinsias de Rossa, whose experiences as a guest of the nation did little to prevent him emerging in the fullness of time as a sex symbol, an MEP, a Government Minister, and the leader of a Party with more seats than Dessie O'Malley.

This period of reflection and study could also explain an admirable flexibility of mind, which would eventually see these implacable Republicans embracing the democratic process with an almost carnal fervour. If Dubliners suspected that Tomas Mac Giolla had suffered for his beliefs and now it was their turn, they were mistaken. On initial inspection, he probably looked a bit too dignified to be the ideal Lord Mayor.

As a rule, dignity is a desirable trait in one's leaders, but a Lord Mayor of Dublin must possess something less than dignity. Because you are called on to behave like a bit of a loodheramawn most of the time, and people laugh out loud when they see you coming, a streak of base populism is a useful asset. If you are not a borderline cretin to begin with, then you have to learn how to impersonate one very quickly.

Mac Giolla appeared a bit bookish, taciturn, a man ill-disposed to performing the hokey-cokey at the opening of Shopping Centres to the strains of the Garda Band. But the record showed that he was not devoid of the common touch. After his incarceration, he received a further blow from the State of which he is now something of an elder lemon. The ESB terminated his contract of employment when he could not guarantee that he would remain outside prison walls indefinitely.

Thrown onto his own resources, he took to demonstrating washing machines, then a relatively new-fangled arrival on the Irish scene. Travelling door-to-door, he would be presented with the filthiest clothes that Dublin could disgorge, and would proceed to give them a spin on the whirly machine. MacGiolla, the visionary of sartorial hygiene, sold very few machines, but claimed to have done the washing for half of Dublin. All jokes about "laundering" and "dirty linen" have been duly noted and recorded.

If you were thinking that he had endured enough for Ireland at this stage, then consider that he went on to sell encyclopedias, a venture which met with a similar response to that accorded the washing machines. The good burghers of Dublin were as omniscient as they were clean. Terrible jobs, but someone has to do them. Was the Lord Mayoralty just the last in a grim series?

No, I'm sure that he allowed himself a warm inner glow as he rested his old bones on the Mansion House four-poster, lay back, and thought about Ireland. And wondered whether they'd locked the doors from the inside or the outside.

WHO ARE THEY, WHAT ARE THEY DOING HERE?

WHAT IS ART?

Incarceration will always be a tricky subject. Perhaps we are looking at the whole issue upside down. Perhaps it is not the case that too many people are in jail, but that the wrong people are in jail. For example, the word "Arts" and the word "crackdown" are rarely mentioned in the same sentence. It would be a brave man who would call for a crackdown on the Arts. But Michael D Higgins is a brave man, and when he became Minister for Arts, Culture, and the Gaeltacht, I sensed opportunities opening up for a new perspective.

At long last, we had a Minister for the Arts who actually knows a lot about Art, having written many stanzas of poetry which aspire to that condition. Shelley thought that poets were the unacknowledged legislators of the world, but Michael D had gone one better. And the possibilities were almost too exciting to contemplate without the close assistance of a leading cardiac specialist.

As a concerned citizen, I drafted a paper of proposals for his attention, and it went like this: He must immediately dismiss the notion that he can be buried under an avalanche of interest groups trying to take advantage of his good nature by bombarding him with outlandish requests and demands for grants, or in the case of the poets, the lend of a fiver. On the contrary, he now has a wonderful opportunity to introduce a more rigorous approach to the Arts, to make them leaner, fitter, and better, and in the process, perhaps even save lives.

In his own field of poetry, it is abundantly clear that National Service must be made compulsory for all people wishing to write verse. I would be more than willing to act as consultant in drawing up a short list of suitable candidates, though this particular "short list" might well outnumber the entire Western Command under the new dispensation. After all, a period in uniform didn't do much harm to the works of men of the stature of Thomas McDonagh, Padraig Pearse, or Billy Bragg, and with a bit of luck, the current breed will learn a more wholesome trade, a bit of carpentry perhaps, which will encourage them to spend less time roaming the pubs, sponging drink off gullible people like me. A spell in the army might be just the thing, as well, for authors of novels which deal with either "gritty, urban realism", or "a young man coming to terms with his sexuality in 1950s Ireland", but this is a less urgent crisis than the poetry.

Street Theatre must be hit hard, and quickly. In particular, there must be a crackdown on Mime, because in recessionary times, there is something basically ludicrous about watching a man pretending to milk a goat on Grafton Street. And the Gardai on this thoroughfare must invoke their full powers on young people caterwauling versions of Neil Young songs, when they should be at home, either doing their lessons or saying their prayers. If they wish to pay for the privilege, fine, but comically enough, they expect you to pay them.

All Performance Art, which is a way of doing things for which most normal people would be arrested, and rightly so, must be met with the threat of appropriate custodial sentences, beginning with six months, and proceeding on to the Death Sentence, imposed by me and a fellow by the name of George.

The Minister must immediately introduce a blanket ban on all Corporate Sponsorship of the Arts. We suffer enough listening to these hyenas telling us that we're living above our means, without having to endure their surreptitious hands up the skirt of popular culture. A quick smack across the face there, and it's over.

Two challenges, above all, await him.

The first is that there should be as many Interpretative Centres as possible, from Ballymun to the Burren. The opposition to these excellent Centres has come from a collection of snobs, wackos and whingers who would deny ordinary, decent American tourists a concise understanding of this fabulous land. People with double-barrelled names and poxy little Citroens with "Nuclear Power, Nein Danke" on the back window, who march into rural Ireland telling the natives how to run their lives. I stand four-square with Ned O'Keeffe TD, who characterised these "environmentalists" as "shouting and roaring like a pack of Balubas", thus bravely jeopardising the crucial African vote in his constituency.

Then there is Temple Bar, the fabled Left Bank of Dublin, where once there could have been a perfectly good Bus Depot. A day rarely passes but I ask myself which is the more important: that a person get home safely to Tallaght in comfortable public transport, or that haircuts with no visible means of support consume Mexican beer by the neck on the pavement in the vague hope of being spotted as an extra for the next Tom Cruise epic?

I am, and always will be, with CIE on this one. The bulldozers, Michael D, the bulldozers. I await his reply.

WHO IS GERRY ADAMS?

Ah, excellent, excellent, excellent. It's the December 1993 instalment of *Esquire,* my favourite magazine. For sexy devils with a big IQ, it is crucial stuff. I wouldn't miss it for the world.

Before reading it, I inhale it. *Hmmmmmmmm.* This month's fragrance is wafting from a Ralph Lauren promotion, entitled 'Safari'. Slap it on and then bag a few tigers. Nice one, Ralph. The *Sunday Independent* should introduce perfumed pages, and then it will be Ireland's best-smelling newspaper.

I take a glance at the ads first, to check out all of the fine things that a fellow in my position might want to buy. I can anoint my body with a tincture of Givenchy, Calvin Klein, Armani, Yves St Laurent, Kenzo, Chanel, or Lauren, skin supplies for men. *Pour homme. Per Uomo.*

I can drive my girlfriends to the Opera in a BMW or an Alfa Romeo, checking the time on a watch by Longines, or Patek Philippe. They can take pictures of me with a camera by Olympus or Minolta. Ah, the agony of choice.

And so to the editorial, the essential brain-food, the articles that are as beautifully crafted as the hood ornament on Eamonn Casey's Lancia. Wearing an all-over spray of gold paint, the cover girl is supermodel Kate Moss. This Moss is a bright lady, who gathers no Rolling Stones. I'll have to check her out.

I like this piece about actor Christopher Walken, the thinking person's weirdo. "He feeds off the idea that he has seen things to which few mortals are privy." Quintessential *Esquire* material. "The thinking man's guide to making the most of your brain", segues nicely into a tribute to Michael Jordan, the man who doesn't have to think, because he can fly.

Then there's this article about Gerry Adams.

Now, have I been drinking my bottle of 'Safari', *pour homme,* or is this a four-page spread about Gerry Adams? Framed against a curiously tranquil backdrop of Belfast, a city apparently pretending to be asleep in the valley below, it is indeed G Adams Esq, sporting a brown ensemble, collar and tie, and immaculately trimmed hair which I suspect to be dyed. Has he dyed for Ireland?

The headline is LOCAL HERO. I know that these designer mags like to splice their high-life coverage with a bit of rough trade, but this is surely one of the genre's most extraordinary moments since *The Face* ran a fashion spread on Lebanon chic, or what the well-dressed Beirut madman is wearing these days.

The Adams fashion-plate is captioned: "Wherever Adams goes among his own people, he is hugged, kissed, and backslapped...but the Shankill blast severely damaged the Hume-Adams initiative".

This indicates the tone of the proceedings, for which we are indebted to super-scribe Emily O'Reilly, who hung out with sexy Gerry in his natural habitats, where everyone wrestled with their consciences and called it a draw. Like Christopher Walken, Adams feeds off the idea that he has seen things to which few mortals are privy.

Martin McGuinness drops by to share the experience: "He talks vividly about fishing, how the night before he had caught nothing, because it was too bright, and the salmon stayed deep down in the pools." I've heard of huntin' shootin' and fishin' before, but this is going it a bit.

It goes on: "There is a picture on the office wall of McGuinness smiling by a river bank, dressed in sludge green waterproofs and tweed fisherman's hat." Meet Martin McGuinness Esquire, angler extraordinaire. As Emily consumes a plain dinner in a "safe house" with the Local Hero, she remarks that "there are few foodie Republicans". Thatcher should have known this when she tried to break the boys in The Maze.

"There is an inevitability about these things," says Adams. "Did you see Bob Fisk's piece about how the public can be re-programmed to accept anything?" Little wonder that he believes in the impossible, as he poses in visionary mode for

Esquire, next door to an ad for Longines watches. Or timing devices, if you like.

He looks terribly dignified next to his near editorial neighbours, Lee Harvey Oswald, and snooker star Ronnie O'Sullivan, whose dad is doing life for murder. With a photo-spread on American deserts, headlined THE DEAD ZONE, and recalling Chris Walken's Russian Roulette game in *The Deer Hunter,* it appears that my favourite magazine has strung together a bit of a theme issue without realising it. These lads are hoors for living dangerously.

It must be a small step now to a *Hello* cover, featuring a photograph of a bunch of lads done up like Keanu Reeves, with the legend, "The boys in H-Block say, we've never been happier." Yet this might prove to be an ill-fated graduation to coffee-table acceptance for The Movement, because when *Hello* comes to call, next thing you know, there's a Split.

For Gerry Adams, everything is now within his grasp, and when Ireland is free, emboldened by his *Esquire* triumph, he might even consider launching his own range of designer scent. Call it Terror. *Pour homme.*

Then it was a case of Meet Gerry Adams...American.

One commentator remarked that with the bagpipes playing, and assorted balubas cheering him at JFK Airport, it was as though Gerry was a local boy who had done well for himself, and was returning in triumph to his home town. Then he departs again for distant Dublin, and he has fellows shouting at him about torture chambers and orphans.

Certainly, the Americanisation of the leader of "Shane Finn" saw him undergo transformations reminiscent of Woody Allen's *Zelig,* who, on account of a bizarre mental disorder, assumes myriad personae in order to fit in with whatever company he encounters. Like Zelig, this "Gerry" person becomes a topic of fevered nationwide debate, and the darling of the talk-shows. But it all started to go wrong for Zelig when his darker side emerged, getting women pregnant by pretending to be Duke Ellington's brother, and so forth.

Whatever way it pans out for Gerry Adams, American (who signed himself into the Astoria Hotel as Schlomo Brezhnev, revealing his Russian Jewish side), he can look back on 'Larry King Live' as the high-water mark of his celebrity. For this hilarious knockabout, beamed into sixty million homes coast to coast, CNN later naturalised him by fitting him out with a real American accent. No doubt the BBC was thinking of exposing the sham of broadcasting restrictions by hiring Sir John Geilgud to declaim the words of Gerry, with Martin McGuinness spoken for by Charles Dance.

The King comedy also featured John Alderdice, as Himself, cast in the role of straight man. Larry called him John Alderice, and they might have developed this gag a little further...Alderice, Aldergrove, Aldermaston, it's Alderbloody same to me buddy !

Larry tells Gerry that Alderice is on the line.

Gerry: "Hullo Jawn, howya doin'?"

Alderice: "We could all be doin' a little bit better..."

Gerry: "Well, exaaactly."

Larry: "Jawn, can't we both agree to stop the killing?"

Alderice: "That's what I would like to hear, but.."

Larry: "Well, you are hearing it. Gerry has said it."

Alderice now trails off from the charismatic duo like a cartoon character blubbering "but, but, but, but..."

Then the voice of the plain people is heard. From Atlanta: "Hi, Gerry, welcome to America. What would happen if the British people pulled out of Ireland? Would there be, like, a civil war between the Protestant and the Catholic?"

Larry: "Would the deaths be worse?"

From Maryland: "As a second-generation Irish-American whose parents were kicked off the farm by British people about 100 years ago, we want peace in Ireland. We want a unified

Northern Ireland." They could have used some canned laughter here, seeing as "a unified Northern Ireland" is not high on Gerry's agenda. Then Larry and he wound it up with a flourish.

Larry: "If we were to come over to Belfast, would you sit down with all the parties and tell the world what's going on?"

Gerry: "Of course I would. I'd also invite you to a pint of Guinness on the Farrs (sic) Road."

Larry: "I won't be shot, though."

Gerry: "No, no, you'll have your pint of Guinness."

But he might be shot, too.

Gerry Adams Esquire is not the only Irish person to raise questions of identity when he goes out foreign. A couple of years ago, I spent an Easter Weekend in London, which, as it turned out, was one of the most "Irish" weekends of my life.

In an Islington pub, a Saturday afternoon *seisiun* grew to alarming and indeed surreal proportions. It was as though everyone who came through the door was handed a musical instrument across the counter, and proceeded to whale away with the ever-growing ensemble. "I'm sorry, we ran out of melodeons an hour ago, would you settle for a jew's harp?"

Wherever I was taken on this strange odyssey, from Camden Town to Elephant and even to Castle, the beat of the bodhran and the scrape of the fiddle saturated my senses, until I had heard more diddley-aye music in three days than for the previous eighteen years. And the set-dancing. Dear God, the set-dancing had reached epidemic levels. All of those nostalgic feasts of Tayto crisps and red lemonade and Marietta biscuits must radically recharge the nervous system so that people drift into a trance from which they emerge hoofing like dervishes, laughing maniacally, lost in a Celtic Neverland.

These were the young emigrants, the notoriously well-educated breed, who, when they lived in Ireland, were pretty unremarkable among their race. They might have been listening to punk rock, dabbling in soft drugs at parties, eating foreign food, drinking foreign drink, and wondering what Iggy Pop is up to these days. Yet now they were learning how to play the tin whistle, and acquiring other adornments of Irishry which they would not have touched with a forty-foot pole in the old country.

They had gone ethnic, and as comedian Sean Hughes put it, they would now do anything for Ireland, apart from live in it. They would be campaigning to free half the prison population where once they would barely march to the shops for fire-lighters. It was all distinctly weird, the way they had integrated happily with Anglo-American culture while in Ireland, and were now detaching themselves from it as they reinvented Ireland abroad.

In Borrisoleigh, U2 had been a bit of a pain in the ass. In Bermondsey, they were the greatest rock'n'roll band in the world. In Carrigaline, The North was bad news. In Cricklewood, the Brits would have to get out, and our law would chucky.

If the London-Irish have a tendency to overdo their enthusiasm for the ravaged homeland, the Irish in America, old and new, regard the first glimpse of Lady Liberty as a trigger releasing a miasma of green imagery which had been deeply buried, and which perhaps ought to have remained buried. Their version of the imaginary Ireland is more intense, the Celtic Twilight suffused with elements of the Clockwork Orange.

We are familiar with the traditional Republicans-in-exile, twisted old sons-of-bitches who think that Dev was practically a West Brit, and who have a disturbing habit of living to the age of 120, kept alive and bellyaching out of sheer badness. We saw the heirs to this bilious legacy indulging in demented celebrations of Gerry Adams and his Pipes of Peace. "Ooh, aah, up the 'RA," they yelled, at gatherings which made a Wolfe Tones gig look like an evening with the Douglas Gunn ensemble. Gerry is a very happy man in this milieu, grinning his ass off, nodding approvingly at the slavering throng. "My people, my people."

In this company, he looks like a god, the way that Fianna Failers in their blue serge suits would dazzle the people of little towns in Connacht with the loveliness of their apparel. As they roar like hyenas for the Brits to get out of "their" country, they are unlikely to borrow a line from Vidal Sassoon — Wash And Go — though on reflection, it's a pretty good one.

Just wash.... and go. In the strangest twist of all, they have a certain contempt for the lesser-spotted Irish who only live here.

What would we know?

WHAT IS JOHN TAYLOR?

A few miles up the road, identity crises are a way of life.

By "a few miles up the road", I mean the place known variously as Northern Ireland, The North, Ulster, The Province, The Six Counties, "Ireland", Britain, Great Britain, the United Kingdom, the Wee North, and Norn Iron. From this multiple-choice selection, I like Norn Iron the best. It is the most representative, taking into account the views of all sides on this island.

At the Edinburgh International Television Festival, the Unionist MP John Taylor addressed the issue of who he was, and what he was doing here. Mr Taylor's efforts at precision in these matters tend to be regarded as mischievous, but if he was trying to wind people up, their reactions demonstrated that he is succeeding.

He accused the media, especially those on "the mainland" and abroad, of bias in their coverage of Norn Iron over a quarter-of-a-century. He claimed that either unwittingly or through preference, they insist on describing the majority British community in Norn Iron as Irish, thus validating the Sinn Fein view that we are all Irish on this island, and must move towards "self-determination."

According to Taylor, they are in fact Scots or Scotch-Irish. And it is a mistake to assume that they live on an island known as Ireland, when there are two countries on this island — the Republic of Ireland and Great Britain. Through this misapprehension, the media, and just about everyone else on "the mainland", choose to regard them as Irish. From where the media are sitting, if in their limited perception, you look like an Irishman and sound like an Irishman, you must be an Irishman, even if you don't feel like one.

But there was more to this than mere shallowness, he maintained. To the media, the British in Norn Iron look like Irish people devoid of the positive attributes of their race, such as a propensity for drinking, cursing, and gambling. While he regards this image of Ireland as a damaging one, he feels that the media are more sympathetic to Nationalists, because in their company, they are more likely to drink, and curse, and gamble. And they like drinking, cursing, and gambling.

Here, Mr Taylor is doing something that is quintessential to the Norn Iron condition: being right and wrong, simultaneously, and eliciting reactions which are both right and wrong, simultaneously. He is right to imagine himself as Scotch-Irish, if he has the papers to prove it, and if that is what turns him on, God love him. Cork people will understand this. They are primarily Cork people, but there are not enough of them to assert this as the mainstream culture in the Republic. This they can only do through hurling, and in the privacy of their own heads.

He is also right to claim that the media prefer engaging with people who drink, and curse, and gamble, but wrong to allege that this is evidence of pernicious bias. It is merely human nature, and perfectly justified when the alternative might involve spending time at some godawful, dour little Orange Hall with a bunch of grim individuals in bad suits by the name of Wesley. Or comforting colleagues who have been turfed out by Paisley after he detected a waft of The Devil's Buttermilk, or even John Barleycorn.

Nationalists will counter-claim an equal bias against them in the media, and rightly so in several instances. Perhaps all sides in Norn Iron can claim a bias against them, and perhaps the bias is valid, the way they carry on their affairs. Nationalists will also resent the drinking and cursing and gambling scenario as being stereotypical, despite the fact that they genuinely reckon themselves to be much better crack than the Prods, more sociable, more free-spirited, more open-minded. They see themselves writing poems and plays and songs, and throwing parties, while Wesley and his God-bothering chums are counting their money, or battering a big drum, or polluting the air with flute-playing.

Most of the parties in Northern Ireland, The North, Ulster, The Province, The Six Counties, "Ireland", Great Britain, the United Kingdom, the Wee North, and Norn Iron, up to a point, have a case to make about who they are, and what they are doing here. The problem is in the way that they make it.

The American writer P J O'Rourke went to Belfast for his book, *Holidays In Hell*. He interviewed a Provo and a DUP man, and thought that in a very broad sense, they were saying virtually the same thing.

He enjoyed himself immensely. And was surprised at how much the locals enjoyed themselves too, knowing how right they were.

ARE WE STUPID OR WHAT?

We have a lot to put up with, like the *Sunday Telegraph* posing the rhetorical question, "Well, Are The Irish Stupid?"

The *An Phoblacht* of the shires was responding to an unfair dismissal/racial abuse case which netted a Norn Iron person some £6,000. It enlisted the help of one Professor Richard Lynn of the University of Ulster to state its case. It omitted to mention that Professor Lynn has attracted protests from the Anti-Nazi League, due to receiving £33,000 from the Pioneer Fund, an American outfit which promotes white supremacy. But it quoted his study of the IQs of different nationalities, conducted in the way that you would establish their average height.

Lynn concluded that we are a bit short of the full shilling when compared to (white) Americans and Britons, weighing in with an average IQ of 95 as against the expected 100. It's official now. We're thicker than the English.

Professor Lynn's theories of racial superiority are based on genetic and environmental factors, and presume that the most intelligent Irish people tend to emigrate, thus diminishing the local stock of grey matter. He cites the examples of Oliver Goldsmith, Edmund Burke, Samuel Beckett and Edna O'Brien. The latter smacks of a pained effort to associate intelligence with the female of the species as well, a case of find-the-lady.

Immediately, one can see a flaw here, as the *Sunday Torygraph* seeks to confirm a few saloon-bar prejudices. What about all the stupid people who emigrate? If you measure the loss of Sam Beckett against the evacuation of, say, two thousand dingbats and a few dozen bozos in the "financial services sector", it all evens up in the heel of the hunt.

It need not be the case that Irish people who become successful while abroad are somehow exceptional. They may merely be taking advantage of lower standards in general. It does not seem to occur to the Professor Lynns and the *Sunday*

Torygraphs of this world that the idea of Terry Wogan being a harmless continuity announcer in Ireland and a cherished celebrity broadcaster in England, may be a poor reflection on England.

Then there is the matter of IQ tests themselves, which most intelligent people regard as proof of little other than the ability to do IQ tests. Like the Bible, they can be quoted in support of all sorts of unsavoury things, and as they operate regardless of race, gender, culture, class, or creed, they are particularly popular on the fascist end of the spectrum, if it needs to be demonstrated that blacks have smaller brains, or that women, God love them, have no brains at all.

Likewise, some of the most obvious cretins on the planet are members of MENSA.

We know for sure that the English character in general is fearful of "intellectuals" in the way that Dracula had a thing about crosses. Irish people, as a result, camouflage their intellect with an ingenious array of feints and shimmies designed to level the playing pitch, a strategy born out of nothing more than common civility, tinged with kindness and a little pity.

IQ tests are reductive, and a bit beneath us, but we are awfully good at things which require a vibrant intelligence, like having parties, building things that don't fall down, brewing, distilling, singing, playing cards, breeding racehorses, and sewing up America. With the brain as with the penis, it is not what you have, it's what you do with it that counts.

Racists and bores cite Irishmen of the navigational bent, who conspicuously abuse alcohol in the pubs of Camden and Cricklewood, displaying scant concern for fresh linen, like Dr Johnson, and talking to themselves in an agitated fashion. Scorning the drab conventions of a make-believe society, you could reasonably argue that by drinking themselves to death, they are doing the most rational thing in the world, embracing the existential demons, jousting with them at the National

Ballroom in Kilburn, as they hear the music of Hell beckoning them into the vortex.

The *Torygraph* can only see what is superficial, libelling an indomitable race from whose loins have sprung Johnny Rotten, Boy George, Chas Smash, Shane McGowan, The Smiths, Elvis Costello and Paul Merton — who have lived among them and saved them from dying of terminal boredom. Those who cross the Irish sea to entertain and enlighten them, they regard as freaks of the herd.

And thus blinkered, they wouldn't even recognise a thick Paddy if they saw one.

CAN WE RISE ABOVE IT ALL?

How do we cope with our own racial stereotypes? A few years ago, some friends of mine were in a taxi-cab in Detroit, and the driver, a black man, asked them if there were many of "the brothers" over in Ireland. Leaving aside the Christian variety, they attempted to compile a list. They mentioned Phil Lynott, and Paul McGrath, and Kevin Sharkey, and Paul Osam and Curtis Fleming who played with St Pat's...oh, and the fellow who plays the guitar outside Bewley's.

"That many, huh?" the cabbie retorted.

There may be an absence of racism in Ireland, but there is also a distinct absence of races, as such. The influential broadcaster Gerry Ryan has ventilated the view that if you scrape the surface of an Irishman, you will discover a mind teeming with images of buck niggers and greasy dagoes and slanty-eyed gets. It's a hard one to call, because it has never really been tested in combat on native soil.

The Chinese and the Italians have found that the way to our hearts is through our stomachs, painlessly integrating by lining our bellies with smoked cod and sweet'n'sour chicken, maintaining a discreet language barrier which discourages drunk people from the usual paths to altercation.

The Italians, being Papist, were away on a hack to begin with. The more the merrier, we all pray to the same God, salt and vinegar, yes please.

As regards the Jewish community, we have consigned the distant memory of the Limerick pogrom to a more barbaric age, and with the absorption of Jews into the middle class, it is difficult to gauge what levels of anti-Semitism may yet linger. Ben Briscoe kept getting elected, somehow, but being Fianna Fail makes him the ultimate ecumenist.

The few Indians among us tend to heal us when we are sick, and for this we are grateful.

Apart from the sporting and rock'n'roll Goliaths mentioned above, such paltry evidence as exists about our treatment of black people usually takes the form of their being denied an entree into the glamourous world of the Rathmines bedsitter. This doesn't really count, because landlords are non-discriminatory in their hatred of all peoples.

What we have here, in effect, is an overwhelmingly, almost absurdly white island. In fact, this may well be the whitest place in the world outside of the Arctic Circle. Our atavistic hostilities are still channelled into tribal and religious warfare, white on white. Even our black protestants are white.

If we do have an ethnic minority, in the sense of an under-class which is at variance with the core culture, and perceived as a threat, it is the travellers. Judging by our masterful handling of this issue, the mind boggles at the possibility of an influx of genuine strangers on the shore. What we know for sure is that our ancestors who fled to the New World tended to view racial segregation in the style of the Alabama police chief who declared that the Nigra problem could be sorted out by a few big men with Alsations.

At home, our insularity has engendered a range of stereotypes which verge on the infantile. Blacks are observed with almost child-like curiosity. A British racist will harbour genuine loathing for the Afro-Caribbean. We just regard them as a novelty, and wonder how they stick the weather.

We see little absurdity in berating Spanish teenagers for conversing loudly in their own language, if you don't mind, and not spending enough money. We, the millionaires and multi-linguists of the new Europe. In a tourist economy, we are either fawning all over foreigners who are passing through, or forming dark suspicions about rich Germans buying up half of Kerry.

Devoid of a consistent dynamic, we divert our underworked racist energies into riotous celebrations of the misfortunes of the

England soccer team. I have seen men weeping with joy, paralysed with pleasure, embracing their fellows with explosive passion, as the final whistle blows on another glorious English defeat. They will always be there for us, and where would we be without them?

There was something uniquely comical about England under Graham "Do I Not Like That" Taylor. It wasn't just that they lost when it counted, it was the knowledge that Graham was going to give one of his laugh-a-minute explanations for the defeat, and crease us up entirely. Wracked with tension on the night that the Republic was due to play Norn Iron in the hell-hole of Windsor Park, I still rang up a friend to whoop and holler when San Marino opened the scoring against England. For twenty minutes, the score line read San Marino 1, England 0, and the idea of England losing to a mountain-top was so fucking hilarious, we were almost willing to accept the wrong result in Windsor Park. The film director Alan Parker was once caught up in one of these raucous celebrations of England's misery. He was hurt and bemused. "But we always support you," he protested. How was he to understand?

One of the transcendent *Hot Press* articles was a piece by Arthur Matthews entitled TEN GREAT ENGLAND DEFEATS, going back to the day that a Larry Gaetjens goal for the USA beat England in Belo Horizonte, 1950, a result which one of the English papers printed as USA 1, England 10, thinking that there was shurely shome mishtake. Oh, how we laughed.

Thankfully, we are not alone in this perversion. When Germany beat England on penalties in Italia '90, it is said that a large group of people marched down the main street of Glasgow singing "Deutschland, Deutschland, Uber Alles". Community leaders said that they were being childish and stupid. Oh, I don't know about that. They were just...enjoying themselves.

When the football season ends, we stay in condition by working out on Spanish students. One of the craziest songs of all time was rendered by Niall Toibin at some sort of celebrity karaoke competition on RTE. I heard it only the once, but it was so magnificently mad that it has remained with me in essence ever since. It is up there with the greatest mad song of them all, 'Thank God We're Surrounded By Water', that joyous, rollicking celebration of in-breeding. And like the Dominic Behan classic, Toibin's gem was a splendid parody of a certain anti-foreigner bias within us.

It was called 'The Spaniard Who Blighted My Life', and for the splendour of its title alone, it deserves entry into some advanced Hall of Infamy. "Life" rhymes with "wife", indicating the nature of the blight inflicted by the Spaniard, and for the climax of this toe-tapping come-all-ye, the balladeer sings: *"He will die, he will die, he will die-diddley-aye-die-die-die-die." Everyone now...He will die, he will die, he will die-diddley-aye-die-die-die-die."*

You can admire the way that the threat of deadly force instantly mutates into the requirements of a drinking song, thus demonstrating that as a race, we would sooner be singing than fighting. But at face value, it serves to encapsulate our general sense of unease with the ways of the Hispanic peoples.

Every year, when the Spanish students roam among us, there are a few little epiphanies which lead me to believe that our way of coping with the bronzed invaders is to try to pretend that they are not there at all. A couple of male Spaniards in their late teens, casually but impeccably dressed, completely sober of course, present themselves at the bar of a South Dublin pub, and order two Cokes. The barman is polite, but he will not serve, though some kind of ID is produced. Exit Johnny Spaniard, browned off.

It is all very silly and embarrassing, but there appears to be a mind-set among the publican class which equates Spanish students with members of the traveller community. The theory goes that if you serve one of them, the whole tribe will be around in ten minutes, annoying the regulars, and shouting at the top of their voices. In a foreign language too, just like the travellers.

Perhaps it's something to do with that old Romany blood, those ungovernable genes which threaten chaos to a settled way of life. Perhaps there's no reason for it at all, other than a gnawing feeling that there should be one. Whatever, it came to my attention that a city centre pub had put up a sign in the front window which read: IRISH ONLY.

It would be wrong to say that we are xenophobic, though in a tourist economy, we prefer those foreigners who look like they are going to throw money at us. We tolerate wretched back-packers from many lands who are by definition penniless, but that's because we feel sorry for them, which makes us feel good, and because they are inevitably going to go somewhere else soon, just because it's there.

We don't feel sorry for the Spaniards, no matter how poor they are. We don't bother to understand that in many parts of Spain, teenagers and even children are entitled to a social life. We don't empathise or engage with them in any meaningful way because we are wracked by an inferiority complex, and rightly so. They are prettier than us, with their beautiful colouring, the ease with which they inhabit their bodies. And that's just the men.

As we sit fuming on the 46A in our sodden, ill-assorted rags, we bitterly resent their boisterous high spirits which lead us to suspect that you don't need drink to enjoy yourself, even though we know for a fact that in Ireland, you do. If they are making too much of a racket, as any bunch of teenagers abroad is bound to do, it never occurs to us to holler, **"Will you shut the fuck up!"** This is not due to some lofty sense of reserve, it's just that we are too repressed to state our feelings in a normal way. And we are further tongue-tied by the knowledge that they have at least one-and-a-half languages, while we, on the whole, have just the one. So rather than indulge our fellow Europeans (hah!) in banter, we silently vilify them just for being there, as we skulk off the 46A in a lather, having gathered more ammunition to share with our bedraggled, malodourous compatriots.

The Spaniards were probably laughing their heads off at the appalling meals concocted by the *bean an tí*, a diet best described by one student who said simply: *"it...ees...not...food."*

The Brits, through the Right Wing of the Tory Party, have found the words to express their pathetic loathing of the browner peoples of Europe, with Michael Portillo leading their chorus of 'Thank God We're Surrounded By Water'. We are content to be remote and sullen. Chances are that the only every-day discourse a Spaniard will have with an Irish person, is with either a head-case or a drunk. The drunks will try to molest them at a disco, whereas I spotted an obvious head-case on the DART, eyes blazing into an innocent Spaniard, asking her "What part are you from?"

It is years ago now since the legendary night in a Dublin bar when a man who was both drunk and a head-case tried to chat up two Spanish women, asking them what part they were from. Keen to display his savvy, he said that he too had been to Spain. And what part, they asked?

"Spain Town!" he ejaculated.

Thus do our two great Catholic nations live and die-diddley-aye-die-die-die-die-die.

ARE WE NICER TO ANIMALS?

Imagine, if you will, that you are a calf. Your mummy takes you aside, and in bovine language, she tells you how to get on in life, such as it is.

She tells you about the desirability of living in a centrally-heated house, where you are guaranteed three good feeds a day. You will have no bad weather, and you're not going to be subject to diseases such as worms or fluke. You are, so to speak, on the pig's back.

This Dr Dolittle performance was staged by one Sam Smyth, a livestock exporter from the wee North, as distinct from the investigative journalist, who exports no livestock. He was explaining to Joe Duffy on RTE radio, that if you could talk to the animals, they would probably choose to live in those much-maligned veal boxes. Animal welfare enthusiasts in the studio appeared to regard this as knockabout comedy of a very high order.

It smacks of that long-running debate about the building of crap bungalows in areas of outstanding natural beauty. They look pretty awful to a person of taste, but you ask the people who live in them what they think, and they'll tell you that these are lovely houses. One person's environmental carbuncle is another person's desirable residence. And anyway, metropolitan nancy-boys and "do-gooders" should mind their own business.

Do-gooders. To the rural sensibility, "do-gooders" are as welcome as mastitis, as pleasing to the eye as rincosporium, as annoying as the mange, the ague, dropsy, or sucking lice. In the war being waged on behalf of calves, the "do-gooders" were winning significant victories, and the farmers were not happy. Officially, the farmers are never happy, but they were even less happy than usual about this.

It must be noted that any cattle controversy at all tends to be bad for agri-business. Whether it's mad cow disease, angel dust, or just "irregularities", chances are that whey-faced town-dwellers are going to switch on the telly and see scenes of cattle in rag order, just when they're sitting down to their tea. They feel bad about the fact that what they are about to receive was once a living cow. The pictures make them barf. They don't like to see their evening meal walking around, swishing its tail, fertilising the land.

In the veal uproar, both sides were alleging war crimes. The laugh-a-minute activists spoke of hideous conditions, of sweet little calves eating their crates, craving fibre. The farmers warned of the end of agriculture as we know it, and thus, the end of Ireland. They claimed that protesters had been reinforced by Lansdowne Road rioters. The latter is surely nonsense. I'm sure that the hooligans were only passing through, and that they would be loath to associate themselves with animal welfare, or any other welfare.

There is an ancient historical dimension as well, with England's problem becoming Ireland's problem. England has a more intense urban/rural divide, best illustrated in the battles over fox-hunting. Here the hunt saboteurs clash with the raddled gentry, the unspeakable in pursuit of the unspeakable. In an ideal world, they would both lose.

Unfortunately, Ireland's moo-cows and their escorts have to run the gauntlet of well-organised protests in England, due to our island status. In what was perhaps their most plaintive whine of all time, farmers could be heard whining about our island status. Certainly, there is a practical difficulty in being surrounded by water, but the farmers can give the impression that this geographical accident was deliberately staged to do them down, and that it demands compensation from Brussels. Or somewhere.

Ivan Yates, the Minister for Agriculture who is all business, went to Brussels, where passions are high. He spoke of a time for action, about state-of-the-art vehicles, about air-conditioning, and all of the creature comforts to which a calf is entitled as its birthright. The Action Man proposes that the journeys of Irish beasts to France be calculated from the time of arrival. The beeves will have a twelve-hour rest on arrival, before being speedily transported to their fate.

Thus, we have a situation in which Irish calves may be exported in better conditions than Irish people. If you have ever taken the ferry on a Bank Holiday, you will appreciate the need for a twelve-hour rest on arrival. Instead of milk, you will have been fed rubber chicken sandwiches and whiskey, and then you will be herded onto a train in the middle of the night, possibly wedged between a pair of soccer hooligans.

You will emerge from this Stygian terror suffering weight loss, fatigue, and dehydration, and if the uncle fails to show up, it looks like there's no alternative but the rough lie-down in Camden Town, in a cardboard box. It will be but a minor consolation that at least you won't be shot, dismembered, sliced into cutlets, and served in gravy. At least not on the first night. If you're lucky.

It is a good thing that cattle will not be treated like cattle any more. But our people require justice too. You can almost hear them moo.

Where The Hell Did They Come Out Of?

What justice is there in a world in which Sonia O'Sullivan can be chiselled out of a World Championship by three Chinese women who appeared to arrive out of nowhere, and who then disappeared back to the obscurity from whence they came?

More than anything else, the Irish love their sport, and they deserve more than just a rake of moral victories to reward their passion. Sonia is now the undisputed queen of the track, but that ghastly night in Stuttgart still sticks in the craw, more so than Eamonn Coghlan always coming fourth in the Olympics. In Stuttgart, too, where Revenge For Skibbereen was finally sealed by Ray Houghton during the greatest England defeat of them all.

Still, the morning after the night before, a couple of elderly ladies on the DART were rewriting history with a subtlety which Deng Xiaoping himself might envy. "Did you see that young girl winning the race the other night?" said one. There was a significant pause for reflection, and then her friend added that "There were those three Chinese girls as well."

"They were working together," the first one explained, displaying a surprising insight into racing tactics. While there was no malice in their assessment of the Chinese performance, they made no effort to erase from the conversational record, the fact that Sonia O'Sullivan had won her race, and that the Oriental contribution was by way of an intrusive side-show.

Wiser heads were saying that Sonia was chiselled out of it well before the race by the sinister medics of East Germany, who are now plying their odious trade behind the bamboo curtain. They thought there was no way that such brilliance could emerge out of nowhere, even if a land containing some 800 billion trillion citizens is not exactly nowhere. They implied that what we had seen was more a tribute to pharmaceutical than to athletic prowess.

Others spoke of masking drugs, and masking drugs to mask the masking drugs. There were objections on aesthetic grounds, because the Chinese did not look sufficiently happy. There was speculation that one of them was actually a man. And anyway, what would "she" want with a bloody Mercedes, isn't she doing alright with a push-bike?

I love this kind of thing, truly I do. We are an awe-inspiring force when we harness all our resources of begrudgery in the national interest, drawing on its healing power to keep the collective dander from drooping. The China Syndrome provided almost scientific proof that begrudgery, far from being a vice, is an ingenious psychological mechanism, a bulwark of self-preservation which we should cherish as an exquisite national treasure.

If we could distil its essence to make us run faster, jump higher, and throw things longer, we would assume permanent occupation of the winner's spot on the Olympic podium, and those East German sleaze-balls could dump their steroids into the Yangtse Kiang for all the good it would do them.

I used to love, too, those gut-wrenching reports of rank injustice being meted out to our amateur boxers, who, for some reason, seemed particularly vulnerable to outrageous decisions by bent Bulgarian judges. Neutral authorities would be dragooned into action to describe "the most disgraceful decision I have seen in all my years at the ringside. And I've seen some, Jimmy." Oh, it was glorious, tigerish stuff, for what is a bronze medal beside an unalloyed moral victory?

Victory is for brutalised nations who practically prise their athletes from the mother's womb to create robotic champions who add a bit of false lustre to rotting regimes. The reason we go completely bonkers when an Irish person actually wins something, is that our mind-set is so attuned to losing in an angelic fashion. Winning in a sense other than the moral one is thus an unnatural occurrence, causing psychic convulsions which are indeed akin to madness.

Post-Sonia depression made us dig deep into our reserves of precious begrudgery, because we had made the dangerous error of actually expecting her to win. Until then, the only person who ever merited such crazed optimism was Arkle, and Arkle was a horse, albeit one to whom we accorded human characteristics. When news of the death of Pat Taaffe came through, I am sure that in a million minds, a timeless, classic image formed of the great horseman aboard the winged Pegasus that was Arkle.

This was certainly the image which rose up before me, and when you consider the fact that I was approximately five years of age when the partnership was at its peak, the impact of their adventures is clearly of the order of legend. I don't remember television introducing sex to Ireland, though I learned later to my delight and occasional consternation that indeed it did. However I do distinctly remember television bringing us grainy moving pictures in monochrome of Pat and Arkle slaughtering the opposition in three successive Cheltenham Gold Cups, and how it was universally acknowledged that these were great days for Ireland.

Perhaps it is that black-and-white memory which makes it seem so special, from a different era, a more innocent time. We didn't have television at home then, but we all piled into the Volkswagon to a relative, who lived a couple of miles outside Athlone and who possessed a primitive model of the beast, to witness the wonder of it all. There were neighbours there too, quietly agog, all eyes focussed on the figure of Pat Taaffe in the pale *geansai* (yellow, I later discovered), with the black hoop, challenging Mill House, the English champion, and doing the business.

It is difficult to imagine it now, but for a good while, Pat Taaffe and Arkle became the very emblem of the nation, as though Stephen Roche and Charlie Haughey had won the Tour de France three years running, or the Republic had actually won the World Cup. It might even be argued that Pat and Arkle were the main thing holding the nation together in some spirit of optimism.

There was no sense of heroic failure here, the gallant Irish in their traditional role of brave and spirited fighters who don't quite make the nut, like being shafted by Australia in the last heave at Lansdowne Road, or Schillaci sending us packing in Rome, or Eamonn Coghlan always coming fourth in the Olympics.

Taaffe and Arkle actually achieved these brilliant victories, and I used to suspect it was because Arkle, being, after all, a horse, didn't have the same psychological pressure as an athlete who would read the papers and get jittery about the weight of national expectations. Pat, however, who like certain supreme sportsmen, always came across as a person deeply unimpressed with himself, said that Arkle was virtually human as regards awareness of a big occasion and the implications. So perhaps Arkle read the papers too, or at least the racing section.

For me, for many years, the name Pat Taaffe was synonymous with his profession in the way that Pele was synonymous with his. I knew that Arkle was trained by Tom Dreaper, owned by Anne, Duchess of Westminster, but I knew that he really belonged to all of us, to the people who sent him birthday cards and presents, and who visited him as though he were a National Monument well after his retirement.

I knew too that Pat had a fistful of Grand National victories and sundry other achievements behind him, but there was something else about Pat Taaffe and Arkle, something else. Charging up the hill at Cheltenham, the rest floundering in their slipstream, commentator Peter O'Sullivan found the right words: "This is the Champion. This is the best we've seen for a long time". — Beautiful winners.

WHY DID PRINCE CHARLES NOT GO TO BALLYMUN?

Before he walked among us, there was talk of Charlo Windsor, Prince of Wales, going to Ballymun. Councillor Eamonn O'Brien, of Dublin Corporation's Special Committee on Ballymun, had written to the Prince of Wales, outlining the benefits of such an outing.

They were many-faceted.

The Prince is deeply interested in architecture, and would probably like to view the monstrous carbuncle that is the Seven Pillars Of Wisdom, in the knowledge that a major £100 million refurbishment scheme is afoot. Councillor O'Brien said that much of the impetus for the proposed visit came from women. While Charlo's record on the woman front is far from exemplary, O'Brien argued that he is a major celebrity, and his presence on the ground would raise the morale of the people. Failing that, they could laugh at him.

There are other reasons why Charlo would find a spiritual resonance in Ballymun, a real sense of belonging. Film-goers will be aware that several Irish motion pictures have portrayed Ballymun as a place where people co-habitate with horses. A place where you are quite likely to meet a horse in the elevator and pass no remarks. Whatever the accuracy of the movie-makers' visions, they would surely evoke powerful images for a Windsor, a breed who are essentially more comfortable with equine than with human beings. For these characters, the words, "Marry me, and I'll never look at another horse", have a special meaning. The women they love may not have been born in a stable, but I'll wager that they were conceived in one.

The Prince is also widely perceived by his subjects as being unemployed, or at least underemployed. He has been mooching around for years, waiting for a job with his name on it. But the system leaves him in a state of grinding frustration, in which the best he can do is keep himself fit, and develop a few hobbies.

Ballymun is full of men in the same boat. They may have had a more humane education, and a more pleasant home life. He, on the other hand, had plenty of "pull" on account of who his mother is. But essentially, they are soul brothers. They could both complain that they have been shabbily treated by the media, and subjected to a lot of public humiliation. All they crave is work. Real work. Not just a stipend from the state to keep them quiet, while they are shunted around from house to house, locked into a meaningless lifestyle.

Charlo Windsor may have more of the folding stuff, but it obviously has not assuaged his misery. He wants to be empowered in a real sense, just like the folk in Thomas MacDermott Tower. The Government has given him a fancy title for official purposes, but there is a sense of sham about the whole business. Howya, sham.

Charlo could certainly relate to the single mothers of Ballymun. He is, in effect, married to one, and is acutely aware of their needs, even if it is only from reading the papers. He could certainly empathise with the single fathers. Like him, they may have been pressurised into wedlock due to social pressure, forced to conform at a time when neither partner was emotionally ready. Now they see their children on a haphazard basis, larking around in a ridiculous fashion, before the bairns are returned to their rightful owners. It is heartbreaking all round, and difficult to receive the blessing of the State to start another family, even if the second union is a happy one.

All things considered, the question was not whether Charlo Windsor should go to Ballymun, but why he would contemplate going anywhere else.

He never made it. No 'mun, no fun.

WHERE IS GUADALOUPE?
WHAT WERE THEY DOING THERE?

"It was the feckin' rum distillery that did it," a Fianna Fail source said ruefully. Fianna Fail sources say a lot of things ruefully these days. Rue, rue, all is rue.

He felt that the proposed visit of Our Men In Guadaloupe to a rum distillery conjured up all the wrong sort of visions of Caribbean merriment. At least the visit to the banana plantation had vague connotations of human toil, and the legacy of slavery. In the context of a fact-finding mission, what sort of facts could our MEPs Gerard "Gerry" Collins, Mark Killelea, Brian Crowley, Pat The Cope Gallagher, Liam Hyland, and, of course, Niall Andrews, find in a rum distillery? That they make rum and that if you drink enough of it, it makes you drunk, perhaps?

Isn't it shocking all the same that we are so insular and riddled with cynicism that we would immediately assume the worst of our MEPs, and jump to the conclusion that they were going out there to enjoy themselves?

According to Mr Blaise Aldo, the Guadaloupe MEP who received the forty-strong delegation, it was all "an occasion of multi-cultural enrichment". And if it's multi-cultural enrichment you're looking for, I can think of no better men to have around than half-a-dozen Fianna Fail MEPs. "Guadaloupe is part of Europe," said Mr Aldo. Technically, he tells no lie, though it sounds like something you would say after seventeen jiggers of Lamb's Old Navy Rum, when the universe itself begins to expand before your eyes.

Mr Aldo has Irish connections in the sense that he is a namesake of "Aldo", the Republic's centre-forward. Multi-cultural connections abound. Why, Guadaloupe is within roaring distance of the lovely isle of Montserrat, where the Irish were transported in chains, and where to this day, their demon seed can be discerned in the red dreadlocks of the locals. Some of them are nearly as Irish as "Aldo" himself. They celebrate St Patrick's Day, they wave the shamrock, and there is an O'Brien on every block.

Once, the Irish travelled in cages. There was no "Europe" then, certainly not in the Caribbean.

On RTE Radio, Mr Wayne David, the Welsh MEP, was in a puritanical lather about it all. "A complete waste of money...scandalous...great shame...reflects poorly on European Parliament...an unadulterated junket." He described the stated reasons for the junket as "a fig leaf", when it might have been more appropriate to speak of "a grass skirt".

'Morning Ireland' noted insinuatingly that none of the Guadaloupe Six was available for comment. Well, it was early in the morning, after all, and by mid-day, Gerard "Gerry" Collins and Mark Killelea were beating the steel drums of vindication, serving up a banana daiquiri of plausibility. Christ, you had to admire their spunk, shaken and stirred with jungle juice, crushed ice, sparklers and an umbrella on top, swizzle sticks on the side.

Collins seemed to suggest that this was a journey taken in self-mortification. He had "felt obliged to accept" the French invitation, and that it was "right for us to show solidarity". Gerard had come to Guadaloupe to share the pain, and to tell them that they were not alone. The macro-political dimension was fleshed out by Mark Killelea, who said that no-one complained when the Women's Rights Committee of the Parliament came to Galway, and were brought to the Aran Islands. While Guadaloupe and Aran are both peripheral regions, some are born peripheral, and some have peripherality thrust upon them. Aran, twinned with Guadaloupe? I think not, sunshine.

He went on to claim that, just like Aran, the people of Guadaloupe have a right to be visited by MEPs. This is pure guesswork, but among the facts you would find on Guadaloupe, I suspect that the right to be visited by MEPs would be rather low on the agenda of public agitation. When it was suggested that six Fianna Failers in the one go was a bit steep, Markeen explained that "we're a broad-minded party". There's no answer to that. Having slapped it into the monstrous regiment of island-hopping women, Markeen then hit out at the goddamn Socialists, 190 of whom were off to Barcelona to celebrate the Brotherhood Of Man, and other 70s pop legends.

The Radicals were packing their bags for French Guyana, fair play to them. Is French Guyana in Europe too? I don't like the sound of it, I must say.

Oh, carry me back to old Guadaloupe.

Who Is Bertie Ahern?

One of the more touching sights in politics is the struggle being waged by Mr Bertie Ahern against the raw material which Nature has bequeathed to him.

As he chases his dream of leading this nation through the new millennium, he has embarked on a course of personal refurbishment somewhat reminiscent of Spenser Tracy in the film version of *Dr Jekyll & Mr Hyde*. I think it was Somerset Maugham who remarked of Tracy's performance that it was very good, only he couldn't quite figure out which of them he was portraying at any given time.

Bertie's quest for the statesman's gravitas arouses similar confusion in the viewer. On 'Questions & Answers', as John Bowman introduced him to the audience, the camera dwelt on a visage which bordered on the funereal. Here was Bertie the grim, ashen-faced supremo, care-worn by the enormity of the burdens which are thrust upon his shoulders as a matter of course, in the high office which he has assumed. It was as though he had been given an injection before the show to freeze his face into a rigid aspect, thus banishing that sheepish grin which we all regard as the chief outward expression of the Ahern persona.

He is impaled on the horns of a dilemma here, because it is the sheepishly grinning Bertie which the public finds most sympathetic. As he formulates the answer to a very hard question, swallowing hard, you are hoping that a fire alarm will go off, or that someone will stage a fainting fit. You can relate to him as a regular guy who is under the cosh. You want to protect him from this torture, take him out and throw a consoling gallon of Bass into him.

The Fianna Fail grassroots, the fellows with the skulls mounted on sticks at cumann headquarters, are confused when they see the sombre Bertrand Ahern. It cheers them up when their boy appears to be putting one over on smart-aleck interrogators like John Bowman, following the party line of "Whatever you say, say nothing."

To the general public, the most agreeable image of Bertie is the one essayed on 'Scrap Saturday', of the new Minister arriving at the Department in an anorak with a Dubs' match programme sticking out of his pocket, being patronised like crazy by the smoothies of Finance.

The anorak is gone now, but he hasn't quite played himself into the sharp suit. You long to see him relaxing at the Budweiser Irish Derby wearing a sponsor's T-shirt, sipping from a plastic cup of the sponsor's ale, and being introduced to visiting billionaires as the...er...Chancellor Of The Exchequer. We are much more comfortable with the idea of Bertie ordering in the beer and sandwiches and stroking the warring factions in an industrial dispute until they purr in unison. In fact, if politics in this country was organised on a rational basis, I think that he would make an excellent leader of the Labour Party, running it in the manner of an old-style Union baron. Unfortunately, the hydra-headed creature that is Fianna Fail has forced him to spread himself a bit thin.

It has at various times, and sometimes simultaneously, been the Party of the small man and that of big business; the Party of social change and social atrophy; the guardian of the Republican flame and the law'n'order Party; the Constitutional Party and the slightly Constitutional Party; the socialist Party and the fascist Party; the labour Party and the conservative Party; the liberal Party and the Party that just loves to party; the natural Party of government and that of coalition; and the Party which thrives on implementing the policies of the Fine Gael Party. Throw in whatever loose spuds happen to be rolling around the political yard, and you have a situation of some considerable confusion.

In a rational arrangement, Dick Spring would join with the evolved wing of Fine Gael to form the Liberal Party. His Socialism was never exactly virulent. No more than his father before him, Dick is not the sort of chap who would curl up in bed at night with the *Collected Works of V I Lenin*.

At that stage, most of the rest of them would fit snugly into a Conservative Party, finally burying their inane animosities.

Under the current dispensation, one can merely detect shades of aesthetic or cultural nuance. When Fianna Failers have sexual intercourse, for example, they are "riding"; the Labour Party are "making love"; the Pee Dees are "copulating"; Democratic Left are "fucking"; Fine Gael are only doing their duty; and the Greens will always have Sellafield.

In the mind's eye, Bertie Ahern is more a man for the smoke-filled room than the gilded banqueting halls of international summits. We see Bertie the ward-heeler, the political mechanic whose electoral machine has caused visiting journalists to gasp with awe, and we are impressed. The real Bertie keeps breaking through the facade, because there are some things you can't cover up with lipstick and powder. And the real Bertie, who will pose with the children of his broken marriage outside Leinster House on Budget day, is no bad thing.

Or at least it wasn't, back in the days before gravitas invaded his being.

The Fianna Failers that Bertie grew up with always had distinctive markings, so they could recognise one another in the jungle. A friend of mine once interfaced with a Fianna Fail member of the Oireachtas, a man who sports a very obvious toupee. To an experienced rug-spotter, all toupees are obvious at fifty paces across a crowded room, but this model was particularly stark, as its owner used to be as bald as a coot before acquiring it.

"It was very strange," my friend recalled. "I couldn't take my eyes off the sliding roof. It got to the stage where all other parts of him seemed to fade away, leaving just the toupee. I was transfixed. Mesmerised."

This endorses something I have believed for a long time, namely that, within the culture of Fianna Fail, the toupee has a conceptual significance which goes far deeper than the mere desire to camouflage a chrome-dome. I even suspect that it may go to the very root of their *modus operandi*.

There, I've said it...root.

If you were to let an apparently innocent little word like "root" slip in conversation with a be-wigged person, you would immediately be stricken by a pang of guilt — " Does he think that I'm trying to wind him up?" Your vocabulary becomes stilted and ponderous, because there are so many ways, however unintentional, of offending a man with a Crown Topper.

"Let the hare sit "...aaaaaagh !

"A horse of a different colour "...aaaaaagh !

The world of language becomes a Cambodia of verbal landmines, all the more so because you just cannot take your eyes off the toupee, and the more you try to steer a safe course of banter, the more your subconscious is slipping you hospital passes, until, like my friend, you are paralysed into silence.

Thus, wearers of the hirsute halo have an appalling kind of power over you, and I think that they are damn well aware of it. I have noted an even more diabolical aspect of the syndrome, the phenomenon whereby certain Fianna Failers contrive *to make their natural hair look like a toupee*. The psychology here is quite ingenious. Apart from the strike-'em-dumb strategy, to the more simple-minded constituents, a toupee signifies that its exponent is a man of such importance that he must take extra care with his appearance. And so successful is he, so much power does he wield, that he can defy Nature itself, and ameliorate the ravages of time with cosmetic ornaments.

The toupee seems to radiate an unearthly, quasi-mystical light, dazzling all who witness it, bringing them to their knees in awe. Whether the rug is real or contrived, it is almost preferable that it looks like a ham-fisted, botched affair, because you want to leave people in no doubt that you are sporting one, and that they are in the presence of Toupee Terror. Then, when the time comes for forelock-tugging, our man can go one better, and whip off the entire thatch, exposing his shiny pate in abject homage to his Leader.

In a remarkable example of serendipity, the Irish-American writer, John Gregory Dunne, over here on a visit, witnessed a farmers' protest outside Leinster House, during which a gust of wind sent a toupee flying across the road, its owner scurrying after it to the great mirth of his fellows. Dunne was only here for a few days, and he had fortuitously stumbled on a hidden world of meaning.

What is to become of this ancient civilisation if even a grassroot of the magnitude of Jackie Healy-Rae is calling for things like nudist beaches? " 'Twill come. 'Twill have to come," he thundered. "In a progressive 1995, when people are able to take money out of the holes in the wall, and jet aircraft can land at Farranfore in Kerry, at the same time we yet have failed to provide a nudist facility on our beaches," he roared.

The Chairman of Kerry County Council was fighting on the beaches of the 'News At One' with Sean McEniff, Chairman of Donegal County Council. Both men are of the Fianna Fail persuasion, and nudism aside, they are friends. The Kerryman dubbed the Donegal man "my very good friend". The Donegalman reciprocated with "my very great friend and colleague". And Healy-Rae trumped this with "my very excellent great friend".

When the oppressive garments of office are removed, and they stand naked in the eyes of their Maker, their two hearts beat as one. Where they differ is on the question of other people standing naked on the shores of Erin.

Healy-Rae was all for it, McEniff was all against it. He felt that in a family resort like Bundoran, the vast majority of patrons would not tolerate people walking around in the nude. But the

Kerryman was pushing the nudist agenda with the zeal of a convert. Kerry was leading the charge on this issue, with a proposal to throw open the Nun's Strand in Ballybunion to naturists from many lands.

For Jackie Healy-Rae, the bottom line is bums on beaches.There are some 30 million naturists in Europe. Why in the name of God can't we facilitate them, and their tongues only hanging out for it? "There is no reason in the wide earthly world why we can't have a little secluded spot in Donegal, Wexford, and every county in Ireland, by going to a little bit of expense," he hollered.

His stance could be described as Pro-Choice. "I am not advocating having these people running wild around the beaches. No way in the wide earthly world," he bellowed. The wide earthly world looms large in his consciousness. For him, there must be no coercion involved. He fumed: "I am not putting one iota of pressure whatsoever on any section of the community to take off their clothes and go nude around the beaches."

I should hope not.

It is all very strange. There was a time when the Fianna Fail grassroots would get into a lather over the thirty-two-county republic, and other such exotica. Now Jackie Healy-Rae, the grassroot's grassroot, is setting an agenda based around two essential forms of liberty: the right of country people to drink and drive, and the right of everyone to spend a day at the seaside buck naked.

There was also a time when a Fianna Fail grassroot would be loath to even go bare-headed in the sun, let alone bare-breasted, or tackle out. A bald grassroot would insist on wearing a toupee as a mark of respect to the canopy of heaven. In these style wars, the big man from Kilgarvan was the ultimate style warrior, training his natural hair to look like a toupee, *pour encourager les autres*.

Would toupees be barred from the Nun's Strand due to naturist dogma? Or would the grassroots argue that the Crown Topper is an intrinsic part of their being, an organic appendage which is part of what they are? Ireland naked is Ireland free, but there would probably have to be a formal issuing of licences to the enthusiasts. Something on the lines of the Rod Licence.

Just remember this when you think of the glory that was Fianna Fail: No man was ever turned away from a cumann meeting because he was having a Bad Hair Day.

A LITTLE BIT OF RELIGION

WHAT DO PRIESTS DO?

Father Brendan Hoban of Killala has described the priestly lifestyle thus: "Most of us seem to spend most of our time answering invitations to social functions, playing golf, breeding horses, training juveniles, celebrating jubilees, pricing cars and reading the death notices in desperation in case we can't get a funeral to attend."

I like it and I think that I might love it. Throw in a few race meetings, the odd sunshine holiday, a torrid romance with one of the parishioners, and you can call me Father Declan.

For some unaccountable reason, Fr Hoban disparages this almost idyllic existence, calling for the Church to be more "lay oriented". Eamonn Casey was lay oriented, and look what happened to him.

The thoughts of Fr Hoban were published in the magazine *Intercom*, and the gist of his argument is that there are too many priests in Ireland, many of whom have so little to do that they wake up wondering how to pass the day. There was a counterblast from the indefatigable Jim Cantwell of the Catholic Press and Information Office, alleging that priests in Dublin are so "stretched", that 30 of the diocese's 200 parishes are run by clergy from Religious Orders. Indeed. I don't doubt that they would want a piece of this excellent action.

Fr Hoban wants the Church to be "less clerical, more user-friendly and more accountable." There is a Progressive Democrat ring to this proposal. "Dearly beloved customers, we are gathered here today..."

It baffles me why some dissident clerics want to spoil it all by getting married, and compromising this bachelor lifestyle with a bit of reality. Consider the pillow talk:

— "What are you doing today, Father Declan?" — "Well, honey, I thought that I might go around to about eight houses for a drop of sherry. Then I'll shoot a few holes at the links with Father Gerry, and later on, I'll probably drop in on the old stud farm. I am the guest of honour at the Chamber of Commerce Dinner Dance this evening, so don't wait up for me." — "Father Declan, you'll have to get a real job soon, you know..."

As it is, things are going swimmingly. The celibacy angle is no problem when you consider the amount of "sexually active" priests. You get to go to loads of weddings, you never have to put your hand in your pocket, and you can inflict your prejudices on a captive audience any day of the week.

"Look what happened to Aer Lingus," Fr Hoban warned mysteriously. As a sky pilot himself, he seems to have a strange yearning for a bumpy ride.

To assist my enquiries into what priests do, I took a boy to Mass on Christmas Eve, because his mother was unwell. No doubt a crown awaits me in a better place. It is fair to say that I could bring to this epiphany a certain sense of detachment, since my experience of Mass-houses has been exclusively confined to weddings and funerals for a long time now.

A couple of years ago, a memorial service for a colleague threatened to degenerate into old-fashioned farce, as the assembled heathens of the mejia, thrown together in these unfamiliar surroundings, attempted to figure out the complexities of sitting, kneeling, and standing, by furtively observing each other's movements. It was a bit like Groucho Marx's famous "mirror scene" in *Duck Soup*.

The Christmas Eve outing would be a less tense affair, because most of the punters were attuned to the procedures, and you would be carried along by the flow, coccooned by protective layers of Catholics. I formed the view that the worshippers at this Vigil Mass were less devout than those who would attend the full-blown ceremony on Christmas Day. This was more like a brisk mile on the flat, compared to the steeplechase which would be held on the morrow.

Anyway, this idea of "getting Mass" at 7 o'clock the previous evening to "do you" for the following day is a bit of a fraud, is it not? I can understand them moving Midnight Mass to 10 o'clock to discourage a lot of drunkards dropping by on their way from the pub for a little bit of religion to "do them", but this 7 o'clock crack is a bit too user-friendly. There was a time when Catholics took pride and pleasure in suffering for their art. Still, this was the Catholic version of the Cup Final, and the church, a drab modern affair, was full to capacity with the fair weather contingent.

It disturbs me more than somewhat that in relation to the modern version of the one true faith, I find myself at various times on all fours with people such as Mena Cribben, Archbishop Lefebvre, and Paisley. Mena may reckon that the present Pope is a dangerous liberal, but she is 100 percent correct about the godawful guitar-twanging which now accompanies the liturgy. I enjoy a good choir, and I like a bit of folk music, but this was neither. Come back *Tantum Ergo*, all is forgiven.

If I am to enter a Mass-house once every ten years, I expect it to look and sound like something more than a pretentious Community Centre. Some churches have even been reduced to hanging kiddies' drawings in the foyer. Churches are supposed to be spooky places, which frighten children with images of grief and piety. They are not supposed to be like a play-school with a touch of naff Simon & Garfunkel, and the occasional endurance test in the form of a letter from St Paul, the Henry Root of his day.

You could fault the late Archbishop Lefebvre and his devotees on the grounds that they are clearly insane, but you have to award them full marks for their espousal of the Latin Mass. This vernacular liturgy is crushingly mundane, allowing the people to participate as though they were worthy. In the days when you didn't have a clue what the priest was saying, though he sounded like he knew what he was doing, you could ponder the mystery of your own ignorance and insignificance, and even say a few prayers. Now you just read a few lines off a sheet with all the fervour of Albert Reynolds reciting the minutes of a Longford County Council meeting.

It was in the sermon, though, where Aughrim was well and truly lost. I think of Paisley — his views on the Papacy are not entirely dissimilar to my own — and his apocalyptic rhetoric, and then I think of this homily at the Vigil Mass, a further example of how the clergy seem determined to ape the achievements of Dermot Morgan in his Fr Trendy phase. It centred around that tortured question, "What is Life Like?", and on this occasion, Life was deemed to be like "a jigsaw puzzle". I will not detain you with the details of this analogy, because you have probably worked them out for yourself, and fast-forwarded to the part where the jigsaw becomes complete with the help of God.

I had a shock of recognition at the enthusiasm with which the congregation rose to declaim the Creed, knowing that they were in the home straight, and it was downhill to the finishing post. This certainly brought me back. Then it was out the door to assemble the pieces of the jigsaw puzzle of Life. We had "got Mass", and the effects of the injection were already wearing off.

For Catholics, things have never been easier. Now, it seems simpler to enter the kingdom of heaven than it is to enter Lillie's Bordello on a busy night. You don't even need to be a regular member any more, it seems.

It was not always thus.

A couple of years ago, at a rocky field near Letterfrack, Co Galway, Mrs Mary Salmon, an eighty-year-old mother of twelve, finally achieved her wish to have the land consecrated. Two of her children were among hundreds of unbaptised babies buried in the plot beside the sea, excluded from the consecrated graveyard due to being in Limbo. For the younger Catholics among you, I could best describe Limbo as a kind of ethereal version of the waiting room at Portarlington station, where the trains don't run. You waited and you waited and you waited in vain, and if there was any consolation to be found at all, it lay in the hope that you would be either too dead or too young to appreciate your predicament.

Limbo, we were led to believe, was as real as Heaven, Hell, and Purgatory. And then they just closed it down, rationalised it out of the celestial budget. "You know all that stuff about Limbo? Well, forget it," they seemed to be saying. It was as though a new Vatican PR department decided that Limbo was more trouble than it was worth. Which is all well and good, and a fine thing all round, as long as you realise that in this, as in many other matters, they are making it up as they go along.

This is not my opinion, it is an eternal truth. Limbo was merely their opinion dressed up as an eternal truth. And then they changed their mind when it suited them. Making it up as they go along.

Like all good things, it had to end some time.

The ferocious public argument about Fr Kevin Hegarty's editorship of *Intercom*, the Catholic Church's in-house magazine, eventually died down. There were reconciliatory noises. It was all very sad.

My days were often brightened by the truckloads of letters to various newspapers, written by angry priests and nuns who were convinced that Fr Kevin had been ejected by his wily superiors for making the magazine too interesting. Then the Bishop of Ferns intervened, admitting that errors and misunderstandings had taken place, and beseeching the clergy to stop writing letters to the goddamn paper. He must have suspected that this was only offering succour to the Church's enemies, and hoped that this succour would not be of the perpetual variety.

Good call, Ferns. Mind you, the same Bishop Comiskey has praised TDs and County Councilors for having their "thumb on the pulse". You can't take someone's pulse with your thumb, because the thumb has a pulse of its own, so you are merely monitoring your own pulse. Is he on to something here as well?

Fr Hegarty was praised for providing "a rare and welcome platform for feminist voices in the Roman Catholic Church in Ireland", and for encouraging dialogue and debate about the issues which trouble modern Catholics in these barmy times. The difficulty with this argument is that if you are interested in the feminist voice, in debate, or even dialogue, the Irish Catholic Church is a pretty bizarre context in which to indulge your enthusiasms.

The more the Pope declares that if you're in the army, you have to wear the boots, the more his free-spirited infantry talk about the need for compassion and flexibility, as though the Church had nothing better to be doing than promoting Christian values. From Venezuela to Ventry, they speak of solidarity with the poor, of the yoke of celibacy, of injustice, as though Catholicism were an exotic branch of the social services.

The Pope inflicts another gruesome old bishop on the diocese, and the Reformers complain about Rome being out of touch with the needs of the community. They become politically active, knowing that the Pope hates politics, which he regards as a synonym for Communism. (Blessing the medals of Latin-American dictators doesn't count as politics, it is just sound business practice.)

This is schizophrenia of a very advanced order (and I don't mean the Jesuits) and now we are offered the scenario whereby members of this mad institution are taking the place of the Left in Irish politics, now that Proinsias De Rossa has curled up in the womb of Government. Proinsias endorsed the Budget, while Fr Sean Healy of the Conference of Religious of Ireland slammed it for its paltry gestures in the general direction of the poor.

The Catholic Church in Ireland is beginning to resemble that legendary movie about Siamese twins, one of whom is a Mississippi racist, the other a black Civil Rights activist. This is quite apart from mutations of the Fr Brendan Smyth variety, and the multitude of sexually active celibates.

It was different with the Church of England, where concern for the wretched of the earth and the role of women relieved the C of E of thousands of crazies and undesirables, who sought solace in the bosom of Rome, feeling that their bigotry would be more amply accommodated under the Vatican code. Good call, Canterbury.

Traditional wisdom has it that the poor are poor because God ordained it so, and that the special genius of women is best demonstrated in the serving of triangular salad sandwiches to visiting bishops. The "loyal opposition", with their meditations on justice and rural atrophy and the desirability of reporting rampant child-molesters to the police, might more aptly be described as "good Germans".

The "good Germans" had little choice but to go along with the antics of the regime, but they tried to compensate in other ways. They wore the uniform, but they didn't actually believe all the bullshit. In authoritarian times, they maintained a conscience, but eventually it was all too much. Like the "loyal opposition" of Irish Catholicism, they had the right string, but the wrong yo-yo.

The disturbing thing about these turbulent priests and bolshy nuns is that they represent some hope of renewal for their benighted organisation. As another Brother emerges from the courthouse on 483 charges of gross indecency, the good Germans come across as personable, articulate, and with most of the attributes of normal human beings. Unlike the original good Germans, their Reich has lasted for 2,000 years, and it intends to continue indefinitely.

I think it's time to form that Escape Committee.

MOTHER TERESA — AN APPRECIATION

The Catholic roof fell in on Christopher Hitchens when he presented a Channel 4 programme venting his spleen at the cult of Mother Teresa. Chris Hitchens argued, reasonably enough, that after a million hours of entirely adulatory publicity, half-an-hour of critical polemic on a minority channel was pretty small beer. He merely outlined her associations with grand old types like Robert Maxwell, the Duvaliers of Haiti, and Enver Hoxha of Albania, and made a reasoned critique of her fundamentalist agenda.

I had gone down a similar road in the *Sunday Independent*, and for some reason, my description of her as a "tough old broad" was the phrase which stuck in the Catholic craw more than any other. For months afterwards, I would see it quoted in anguished tones as a kind of landmark in depravity. They obviously missed out on Eamonn McCann's " wicked old crone". The article arose out of the refusal to allow Mother Teresa to address the nation in the context of the Oireachtas. It seemed like an astonishing decision, until you examined the motives which informed it. However dreary they may be, the people who allegedly run the country know a little bit about power. They can recognise a serious power trip when they see one, and Mother Teresa is about Power beyond the wildest dreams of any of these people. There was also the fact that she would undoubtedly use the platform to rail against contraception, divorce, abortion, and anything else which stands in the way of Catholic breeding rituals. They would probably have to give her a standing ovation for this, and generally go belly-up in her presence, and all round, it would not be a pretty sight.

"Why are all these grown politicians so afraid of a little eighty-year-old nun?" her supporters cried.

There are eighty-year-old nuns, and eighty-year-old nuns. But the little Albanian eighty-year-old nun who visited our shores just happens to be the most popular Catholic in the world. To describe her as merely an eighty-year old nun was like describing the Admiral of the Fleet as a jolly sailor boy. With John Paul II losing the lustre of stardom, she is the Sinatra of the fundamentalist lyric, crooning the toons just right, all the nuances in place, the wave of the hand, the way to work a room with one flicker of expression, the sense of command, and the timing, the timing.

She is also a Saint.

This is because of her work with the wretched of the earth, which Chris Hitchens claimed was not all it is cracked up to be. Few people have done more to encourage a belief in the beauty of poverty, as they travel First Class on aeroplanes around the world, spreading the message. In 1975, she said: "Some fight for justice and human rights. We have no time for that." She thinks that people just need a little bit of religion, a final leg-up on the way to the cemetery, at which point they will enter a far better world, in which, their souls newly polished, they will be ecstatic for an eternity of Catholic heaven.

Her devotion to the poverty imperative is such, that she has successfully interfered in UNICEF family planning drives in the Third World, in order to bring them more into line with "Catholic teaching". I would have thought that with the problems they have out there in Africa already, the Billings Method is just about the last straw, but I am sure that she is proud of herself.

For an avowedly celibate woman, she has a mania for persuading other women to have enormous amounts of children. I sensed a flaw in this rhetoric when she said of Prince Charles and Lady Di, in the early years of their "marriage", that "two children are not enough. They should have five now." There, but for the grace of God...

In Ireland, she resumed a long-standing theme of hers, whereby she will "adopt" children born into degrading squalor, and find them decent homes of the Catholic persuasion. Yes, the punters love a good fairy tale. I can see it all now: "Don't worry, little Jason, your thirteen brothers and sisters will look after you, and if they can't, I'll send you over to Mother Teresa of Calcutta. And then you'll go to heaven."

For a long time now, her poverty agenda has been lagging well behind her devotion to travelling the world, putting lead in the pencils of " pro-life" movements from Brighton to Benghal to Belfast. The Pope loads the gun, and she pulls the trigger. Mother Teresa, The Enforcer.

Her official canonisation will be a formality. If you can look at Mother Teresa and see "a kindly old nun", it is a miracle in itself.

FR MICHAEL CLEARY — AN APPRECIATION

I used to hear Fr Michael Cleary's show on 98FM most nights. There was an elderly woman living beside us who was almost totally deaf, and who used to play it at massive volume. At ten o'clock each night, this ghostly sound would seep through the walls, as though he were haunting us. For a laugh, we would debate whether to ask her to turn down the racket for the sake of the child, but life was too short.

The show was a kind of extended Parish Bulletin. There were greetings from prisoners in Mountjoy and Wheatfield. One night, Cleary inadvertently read out a note to a prisoner from his (the prisoner's) girlfriend, saying that she couldn't stand it any more, and she was leaving him. That must have livened up the proceedings in D-Wing. What sort of crime would you have to commit to receive a 'Dear John' letter from the mouth of the Singing Priest?

He interviewed a lot of people who would give out about "liberals". Youth Defence got their first big break courtesy of Fr Mick.

Then he would go home. To his wife.

By two o'clock on the day that *Sunday World* printed its Father Mick extravaganza, you couldn't get a copy of the paper for love nor money. Amazingly, on RTE's 'The Sunday Show', Ronan Collins was wondering what was the point of publishing such a story at this stage? Well, Ronan, the fact that Ireland's most famous priest, the warm-up man for The Pope (him and Eamonn Casey), was married-with-children for twenty-six years, is, I believe, of some passing interest.

Ronan regretted that Cleary wasn't around to defend himself. I deeply regret this too. Like Russell Murphy and Robert Maxwell, the old fraud effectively got away with it. Still, there's a lot to be said for lying out in the garden with the sun blazing down and a bottle of beer in your paw, listening to another clerical scandal unfolding on the wireless. The sound of Summer.

Bishop Thomas Flynn went into denial straight away, a traditional posture later adopted by a representative of SPUC, who suspected a conspiracy. But of course. These people believe in eternal life after death, but they don't believe that Fr Mick was sinking the pink? Planet Earth calling, Planet Earth calling...

The dogs in the street knew about Cleary, but dogs in the street are not a reliable source, unfortunately. Cleary was as meticulous as The General in assembling alibis. He lied to friends and relations, he organised affidavits, he bullshitted about charity and Mary Magdalene, he even did a DNA test for issue that was not his, a bit like a Government Minister chuckling to himself because the Opposition asked the wrong question.

To make it stand up on its hind legs and wag its tail, you needed the Annie Murphy Factor. Cleary's little mafia of clued-in friends and associates must have been banking on the fact that Annie Murphy was a one-off, a very American kind of outrage. Would any dacent Irish woman, imbued with the faith of our fathers, blow the gaff like Hurricane Annie? She would, and she did, for her own good reasons, and those of her son, and reasons which remain in the realm of speculation.

Anticipating a deluge of denial, *Sunday World* threw in the Ivor Browne Factor, to be sure, to be sure. With written permission from his patient, the mother of Cleary's children, the distinguished doctor confirmed the story, and said that he could fill many newspapers with the havoc wreaked by the Mickser Clearys of this world. The Man Who Shouted Stop was then blackguarded on grounds of ethics. This was becoming an orgy of denial. If they couldn't accept such overwhelming evidence about something so relatively trivial, what chance was there of Fr Brendan Smyth having his collar felt?

The word "tragedy" was freely kicked around as the RTE switchboard was threatened with meltdown. "Farce" is ultimately a more accurate description. This was farce heaped upon farce for a quarter of a century. It was farcical to a medieval degree. It was as farcical as Farcical Jack McFarcical, Professor of Farce at Oxford University. This ghastly chancer, the most vocal reactionary in Catholic Ireland, married with children. Hypocrisy doesn't come into it when you contemplate Farce on this scale.

The weekly poker sessions in which he would take a tenner out of the pot for "poor oul' Phyllis", who provided the buffet for the players. Is this cheating, or is it just low Farce?

We are encouraged to treat Irish clerical controversies with much seriousness, when it looks increasingly like something thrown together by Brian Rix, farceur extraordinaire. But above and beyond all this, there was the spectre of a thirty-seven-year-old hard-chaw telling an extremely vulnerable seventeen-year-old girl that before the time of Christ, a couple could exchange marriage vows in private. These vows would only be recognised by God when the "marriage" was consummated.

I tell you, there are fellows below in Leeson Street with twelve pints and four bottles of Blue Nun inside them, who would not descend to this level. Well, they might, but they'd hate themselves in the light of day. Cleary, the control freak, didn't even have the benefit of being stiff with drink when he emerged with what must be one of the most atrocious lines in the history of human seduction.

By the way, can you get divorced just as easily? Apparently not.

Of course, Cleary abominated Leeson Street, telling an interviewer that he could go down there any time and "pick up a woman" if he wanted. Which he didn't, being above all that. The photographs which accompanied the interview bore eloquent testimony to the man's indomitable neck. Would that we were all so cock-sure.

When I wrote about the living Cleary, I would dub him "Father" Cleary for a bit of diversion, and the *Sunday Independent* sub-editors would duly whip out the inverted commas. Harmless amusement, God knows. No need for that now in the case of Mick Cleary, father-of-two. And counting.

In an odd way, you'd think that Churchmen would be relieved to move the debate away from child-abuse, and into the knockabout realm of "priestly celibacy". But no. The following week in *Sunday World*, Fr Brian D'Arcy was not a happy camper. The man who loves to laugh was in bellicose form as he shot the messenger full of holes, the messenger being his own splendid organ, to which he has contributed for nineteen years. It was a little bit of religion, and a whole lot of blood on the galleys.

"Fr Michael Cleary has had his corpse picked over by a marauding media," he wailed. "He has been callously maligned without a right of reply. He has been labelled a hypocrite by sometimes sneering, lewd people." This is emotive stuff, combining images of necrophilia with the language of the Hugh Grant debacle. A little bit of lewdness goes a long way.

High on emotion, he lashed out at phantom enemies: "I have been torn to pieces for daring to say that dead men cannot defend themselves." Sad but not true. It requires no daring to say that dead men cannot defend themselves. It is a mere statement of universally accepted fact. And I scoured the marauding media in vain to find any evidence of Fr Brian being torn to pieces, or even exposed to mild rebuke. Not a sausage.

He wrote that he had also been torn to pieces for "telling the truth — namely that Michael Cleary vehemently and adamantly denied those very rumours on many occasions to me whilst he was alive." This may be factually correct, but a tad misleading. Cleary's denials to him were *a* truth, but not necessarily *the* truth. In terms of priority, the larger truth was that, on the overwhelming balance of evidence, Fr Michael was talking through his d'arse.

Avoiding all that unpleasantness, Fr Brian insisted that "I believed Michael Cleary when he repeatedly denied the rumours to me whilst he was alive, as recently as three weeks before he died." As Confessor to the show-band community, Fr Brian must have heard a few whoppers in his time, but why was it necessary to *repeatedly* seek denials from his good friend? I mean, would once not be enough? Twice, and leave it at that? Under that kind of interrogation, it's a wonder that Cleary didn't confess to the shooting of Michael Collins.

But the Singing Priest was made of sterner stuff, refusing to sing under the rack of the Inquisition. Sneering, lewd people will say that he refused to squeal on himself, but Fr Brian attributes far higher motives to his fortitude. Again, he got it straight from the horse's mouth: "He was annoyed at what the rumours had done to him, but he was even more devastated when he saw the impact they had on Phyllis and Ross. The hurt they endured broke him. But he made sure, whilst he was alive, that they were protected from hurt and harm." As for the provisions in his will, Cleary told his good friend: "I cannot allow evil gossipers to stop me doing good."

Oh, Father, aren't you the right one?

High on the improbability of it all, Fr Brian maligned Phyllis and Ross: "I can't believe that they would want to do such a thing to him in death," he storms, but a few paragraphs later, he is conciliatory: "There are many other things I could say, but I would run the risk of breaching confidentiality. I do not wish, at this point, to be destructive to any living person. Enough hurt has been done." Like his good friend, Fr Brian wants to have it every way.

He was incandescent about his own organ, slamming, and indeed lashing the editor for failing to grant him the courtesy of a simple phone call before publication, "as I believe my involvement with all sides in this sad affair was generally known."

But sure, life is like a box of chocolates. You never know what you're going to get.

THE BIG PICTURE

Let us raise our eyes from these earthly woes for a moment, and contemplate issues of The Eternal. Even that is not what it used to be.

Recently, I have been seeing God in the most extraordinary places. There is a growing body of evidence that either God has discovered rock'n'roll, or rock'n'roll has discovered God. This is quite a departure from the script we were given as bairns, but it is becoming increasingly apparent that some very serious contemplation of the Almighty is taking place among practitioners of popular culture.

As another Catholic priest emerges from the Four Courts wearing a motorcycle helmet to shield his identity, people like Samantha Fox and Eileen Reid are speaking about their deeply rewarding relationship with the Creator. As surly old bishops blather on about contraception, Christy Dignam of Aslan tells *Hot Press*, "I've spent a long time looking for answers, and until I find some that satisfy me, I'm always going to have this God fixation." Elsewhere in the same issue, Michael McGlynn of Anuna says, "If I believed that what I write comes from myself, then I would have no reason to live...it has to come from somewhere, whether it be a God or an untapped energy that runs through every living creature."

As Cardinal Daly despairs of those clerics who are unable to mingle with children without buggering them, Pearse Turner tells Joe Jackson in the *Irish Times* that he wants to reclaim a hymn like 'Faith Of Our Fathers', and encourage people to sing it in pubs. As the fundamentalists brandish their dismal pamphlets, the likes of Liam O'Maonlai, David Byrne, Gabriel Byrne, and B P Fallon are talking on television about the mysterious sources of their inspiration, their dealings with the intangible. And Van Morrison, Bono, Larry, and The Edge (but not Adam), have been plugging in to the celestial switchboard for a long time now.

So what is going on here? With the possible exception of Eileen Reid, none of these people are exactly renowned for their regular Sunday devotions at the kirk, or their allegiance to one of the world's great religions. Several of them specify their antipathy to such practices, as though they were an unsavoury distraction from deeper contemplations.

In Ian MacDonald's book, *Revolution In The Head*, he argues that the incredible appeal of The Beatles was based on a "spiritual crisis" looming in the West ever since the age of the Enlightenment put God out to grass. John Lennon's comment about the Beatles being bigger than Jesus Christ was a simple statement of fact. Rock'n'roll can trace its roots back to Gospel music, and thousands are satisfied that in Elvis, Dylan, Clapton, or Paul Hewson, the plan of the Almighty can be discerned. They light candles in their presence. It seems that a lot of people are coming around to the view that there is more to this than craven hero-worship.

They say that one basic difference between the Right and the Left is that the Right uses religion to let off steam, while the Left chooses Art. Now, the lines are becoming more blurred, with Tony Blair talking a lot about Christianity, and John Major trying to explain away all those weekends in Paris. Is something similar happening on other fronts, with hairy musicians describing their conceptions of the supernatural, while Catholicism sinks into a black hole of sleaze?

There may be more prosaic reasons for this eruption of speculation about forces beyond our ken. The end of the century has a tendency to make people come over all funny, seeing apocalyptic visions in strange places, willing some sort of resolution to major metaphysical issues. In crude terms, a lot of rich sinners may be trying to get on-side before the balloon goes up.

There is also the question of Ego, a commodity which musicians and actors have in abundance. The fact that they occasionally see God when they look in the mirror may be fuelling their curiosity. Certainly, a lot of cool customers are seeing the Light, and are telling anyone who cares to listen. The traditional agents are just seeing a mountain of legal bills, and the end of their world drawing nigh.

Let us go even further back, to the primary sources, as it were. Thanks to our excellent educational system, we Irish have long ago dispensed with enquiries as to the origin of the Universe. "Who made the World? God Made the World." It took him six days and then he had a rest. But the scientific community is still tinkering with the why's and wherefore's of the Creator's handiwork, and I suppose we must humour them in their innocence. A couple of years ago, they became rigid with excitement at discoveries made by NASA's Cobe satellite, which detected "ripples", giving a kind of fossilised impression of the birth of stars and galaxies.

This birth occurred fourteen thousand million years ago, so while it is not exactly hot poop, it offers reasonable copy on a slow day at the News Desk. The formation of galaxies has always puzzled the experts, but now they have established that it all came about some 300,000 years after the Big Bang which caused the Universe to come into being in the first place. And who caused the Big Bang? Answers on a postcard, please.

There is considerable beauty in the scientific quest for such information, but surely there is a more romantic beauty, even a touching humour, in the notion that Adam and Eve's Little Bang was the event which really got the ball rolling in earnest. Still, subscribers to religion must be feeling a small twinge of apprehension at what the Cobe craft is likely to uncover as it continues its voyage. It has made 300 million measurements since its launch in 1989, and now that it has discovered the Holy Grail of cosmology, who knows what awaits around the next celestial corner? I know a lot of people who would not care to open their newspaper and read a headline saying: COBE LATEST: HE'S NOT THERE AND HE NEVER WAS...(see Editorial, "Goodbye To All That").

Yes, there will be doubters. Darwin, after all, is still considered to be something of a quack and a troublemaker by certain important people, not least the former President of the United States, Mr Dutch Reagan. You may argue that the NASA boffins would be better off down on their knees saying their prayers. Or maybe you don't want to think about it at all. Around the time of Cobe, various authors were releasing updates on the life and career of Jesus Christ. His followers will doubtless be interested to learn that there was no Virgin Birth and no Resurrection, that Jesus married Mary Magdalene, got divorced, re-married, had three kids, and lived into his seventies. This is the way that theologian Barbara Theering reads the Dead Sea Scrolls. In her book, she would contend that the disciples tricked the Romans into believing that Jesus had died on the Cross by administering poison to him. They then revived him with medicine, and he continued about his Father's business in the manner outlined above. Good luck, Barbara, you're going to need it.

A N Wilson was pitching in too on the No Resurrection/No Virgin Birth ticket, adding *en passant* that Christ had no interest in starting a world religion, particularly one named after himself. He just wanted people to be better Jews. The world religion bit was St Paul's idea. No great lover of women, he may have felt that "Christians" has a better ring to it than Paulines.

Then Dr Luigi Malcantraco ascended the podium with a book which claimed that Jesus was effectively dead at the Crucifixion, having suffered a massive heart attack in the Garden of Gethsemane. He stands by the Resurrection, though I would be interested in hearing the views of a medical man on the Virgin Birth. It's a puzzler, for sure. Meanwhile, Mr Gore Vidal was working on a novel, *Live At Golgotha*, in which, *inter alia*, Gore assumed the narrative persona of St Timothy, and conducted a homosexual affair with — it's that man again — St Paul. Gore's publishers would have to talk very sweetly to get a window display in Veritas for that one.

Returning to earthly science, Dr Brendan Healy, President of the Irish Hospital Consultants Association, and Severino Antinori, a controversial gynaecologist, spoke on RTE's 'News At One' about Dr Antinori's policy of helping women beyond the standard childbearing age to have babies. These tend to be rich women, or women with rich husbands, who have pursued a successful career, and who now want a child, though they may be in their late 40s, 50s, or even 60s.

Dr Healy spoke darkly about the need for women to have children when they are young, to assist the bonding process, and he was uneasy about the concept of older women having a baby just because it is handy for them now. Ethically, he was dubious about "discarded embryos". You have to imagine what women feel, as distinguished male medics wrestle with these "ethical" problems on their behalf.

Dr Antinori seemed like a right card. He has worked on the "salmon effect", whereby spermatozoa swim against the current of the seminal fluid, like salmon swimming upriver. His findings have been hotly disputed. I know the feeling, and so do my spermatozoa. With Cyril Cusack playing the medical mandarin Healy, it would have to be Peter Sellers in Italiano mode, as the emotional Antinori.

When the man from RTE proposed that his procedures were "totally unacceptable", he said something like this: *"Ethical problem, ees no important. Because I work for de weemen in good condition. I ask another question to you. When five meelion people aborshoon in Oorope, ees ethical problem? No! Not a way."* On the subject of the "discarded embryos", he said something like this: *"No! No throw away. Nothing. We receive de donor outside from weemen, anonymous. De patient with de sperm you 'arbour...but no, no throw away! Meelions aborshoons in Oorope. So what do you reespond? We killa de baby weeth aborshoon. I don't killa de baby!"*

He is a religious man, withal: *"I am a Catholeek. We musta remember de Pope. There ees a right to life. Ees OK, when eet is possible..."*

The man from RTE claimed that De Pope is dead against this idea of women having babies just because they feel like it.

"De Pope, de Churches agree with me because I am for life, and not for aborshoon. Fine, there is the killer in England, in America, in Eengland. We must fight dees killer. Thanka you very much !"

Be careful out there.

PHEW! ROCK'N'ROLL

THE CROCK OF GOLD

With me and Albert Reynolds, you always get it straight. That's how you get it. Straight.

So I'll tell you straight now, before we go any further, the way it is: I'm more of a De Dannan man than a Chieftains man.

When Frankie Gavin and the lads are going at it full tilt, something shudders in the bowels of the earth. De Dannan are elemental, tearing off a tune with a built-in swagger that brooks no opposition. They would cream an audience of dead Methodists.

Paddy Moloney's men don't do that voodoo for me. Oh, I know only too well the depth and breadth of the musicianship among them, but I also hear connotations of the stately home, the medieval castle, the minstrels summoned by his lordship to pleasure him. In the great hall, he takes his ease after a bout of rape and pillage, oak tables groaning with haunches of venison and flagons of mead and buxom wenches, his savage breast becalmed by the artistry of Moloney and his merry band.

The potentates of Nineties Rock are similarly beguiled by the Chieftains, and never more so than on their extraordinary album, *The Long Black Veil*. Weary from their latest corporate adventures, their plunder of musical territories throughout the globe, they bank their booty and then chill out to shake their booty with Ireland's fabled ambassadors of *ceol* and *craic*. Sting, The Rolling Stones, Mark Knopfler, Tom Jones (Tom Jones!), they're all here. Van Morrison, Sinead O'Connor and Marianne

Faithfull have never really been away. And Ry Cooder drops by to make it a truly international *craic*-fest.

In the land of the Chieftains, they can get back to their roots, or at least to somebody else's roots. They can stretch out and enjoy themselves in the knowledge that they won't have to run this stuff past their accountant. Meanwhile, Paddy Moloney's accountant is delighted to have them on board, and a great time is had by all. I believe it's called "a sharing of musical ideas".

The results of this jolly fusion are both pleasing and alarming, sometimes simultaneously. Sting, singing *as Gaeilge*, for Christ's sake, makes a magnificent horse's collar of '*Mo Ghile Mear*'. Now, I'll tell you straight, because you always get it straight from me, I love this number. A blast of this from Peadar O'Riada and the Coolea Choir and by jaysus, boy, you wouldn't know yourself. From the throat of Sting, you know why he called himself the King Of Pain. I hope he isn't equating Paddy Moloney with that Amazonian friend of his with the saucer in his lower lip, and doing another bit for an indigenous people threatened with extinction. By the sounds of it, he needs us more than we need him.

Jagger, who shares with the Chieftains an interest in all things Guinness, essays his Ned Kelly impersonation on the title track. 'The Long Black Veil' is a dark and mysterious spine-chiller when Robbie Robertson and The Band are singing it. Jagger just sounds like he's acting the tool. But such are the magical healing powers of the Chieftains that he winds up on the same album as Marianne Faithfull, united once more under the Celtic moonlight.

Marianne does a grand, bitter-sweet reading of 'Love Is Teasin', fair play to her. Mark Knopfler also escapes by the skin of his teeth with 'The Lily Of The West', and Ry Cooder is characteristically sublime on 'Coast Of Malabar'. Lovely hurling, Ry. And Ry-fol-de-daddy-o.

Van The Man thickens the plot with another version of 'Have I Told You Lately That I Love You?', the amnesiac's anthem. He has asked this question before, but he didn't have Paddy and the Boys with him at the time, so I suppose it's worth another lash. Photographed with the Chieftains in their vintage 1950s Civil Service rig-outs, Van looks like a bit of a dandy. It is said that Van and Paddy once solved a lingering dispute by pouring a bottle of wine over one another's heads. A touch of sartorial rivalry, perchance?

Sinead O'Connor slaps it into Johnny Brit one more time with feeling on 'The Foggy Dew', and does a beautiful 'He Moved Through The Fair'. Usually it is "she" who moved through the fair. In changing the gender, Sinead draws our minds to the fact that men who move through an Irish fair are not exactly ideal material for paeans of romantic yearning. Spitting on their palms, checking the teeth of horses with a gnarled paw, and celebrating a done deal with torrential waves of porter, they do not readily invite metaphors of the swan on the lake at eventide.

Enter Tom Jones (Tom Jones!) in the final furlong, a Celtic soul brother, with a killer 'Tennessee Waltz'. What a wonderful song it is, and how remarkable that Tom emerged from the Vegas years with his *cojones* in such working order. The man must have more testosterone under his belt than the entire Bulgarian Ladies Shot Put squad. They will have to do this one on stage, so that we can see Derek Bell's expression when items of lingerie intended for Tom's brow start landing on his trusty oboe. Can Paddy's pipes function under a hail of crotchless knickers?

Speaking of which, The Rolling Stones conclude the festivities with 'The Rocky Road To Dublin', about which nothing need be said other than thank God for the Mullingar by-pass.

Craic? There's nearly no other word for it.

GARTH BROOKS — PRESIDENT OF THE UNITED STATES?

There is talk of Garth Brooks going into politics.

If he does, I can't see much stopping him becoming President of the United States.

He could stand for election virtually unblemished by past embarrassments, because the place he is coming from — the industry of human happiness — is one of the last areas of public life which the masses perceive to be a force for good.

The culture which now amusingly describes itself as "rock'n'roll" has imploded to such a degree that it is bereft of its single most useful purpose: the giving of bad example to the young. Not only has rock reneged on its responsibility to lead the youth astray, it has set its compass firmly towards the high moral ground, with its disavowal of drink, drugs, and bizarre sexual practices, and its shameless espousal of charitable works.

There was a palpable hysteria in the 'Kenny Live' studio as Garth Brooks appeared to the many in Montrose, radiating goodness. I spotted at least two of RTE's head honchos in the audience, abasing themselves like ordinary punters, touched by the sanctifying grace of the Oklahoma Kid and his 300 million bucks. It was sort of pathetic, but then the honchos may have sensed a shift in the moral universe, and were paying homage to a world leader of pop in the way that they would traditionally fawn over a President or a Pope.

Garth's reconciliation with his wife after a period in which he had been a "bold boy" — a very, very bold boy from what one can gather — somehow magnified his goodness, his reaffirmation of family values. And when he cried....oh, man, when he cried. Big Tom is a sentimental guy, but he never cried on television.

The country stars who have preceded the teetotal Brooks did a lot of crying too, men of genius like Hank Williams and George

Jones. But their tears were a natural consequence of the monstrous levels of substance abuse and bad craziness to which they were devoted. In addition to writing immortal songs which make the Brooks oeuvre sound like Pat Boone on steroids, they fulfilled the equally important function of being execrable role models, setting standards which it would be almost humanly impossible to live down to. For all this, they are rightly hailed as collosi.

Mr Hank Williams once drew his gun in a restaurant and shot a painting of a battleship, because he was sure the ship's cannons were going to get him first. Good call, Hank. Mr George Jones had his car-keys confiscated by Ms Tammy Wynette to stop him escaping to the honky-tonk, so he climbed aboard a lawn-mower, and in this stately carriage, old George made his way to the oasis. Nice one, George. Mr Ronnie Hawkins once told the great Robbie Robertson that he couldn't promise him much money, but he would get more pussy than Frank Sinatra. Ronnie boasted of knowing "every backside and back-alley, from Newark to Mexicali". There was no reason to doubt it. And I attended a press conference in which Johnny Cash was asked, "John, is it true that you were once dead for forty-five seconds?" Golden moments.

Now the multitudes raise their howdy-hats to acclaim Garth the Good. Brooks is a potent example of the creeping Jesusry which has decimated the unruly spirit of rock'n'roll, as its beaming ambassadors lurch around the globe on endless mega-tours, making benevolent noises whilst avoiding anything which resembles a contentious comment. For a while, Adam Clayton was trying to revive the rite of extravagant behaviour in hotel rooms, but he showed no stamina. Michael Jackson doesn't count, because he is too mad to relate to.

The upshot of all this purity on board the rock juggernaut is that when the youth of the world look to people who can show them bad example, they must look to politicians, lawyers, footballers and bishops. In these areas, you will find the ragged remnants of what used to be known as the counter-culture.

There is scarcely a politician on the planet at this moment who doesn't emit little rays of sleaze from his personage. Lawyers are openly greedy to a reckless extent. Diego Maradona snorts cocaine by the barrel and athletes are doing drugs which will probably turn them into baboons at forty, but what the hell. And bishops are being sized up both as holy men and as hammer-men.

Sleaze, greed, drugs and kinky sex practices abound in milieus which were once thought respectable, while the avatars of taste in these fields, the Jaggers and Bowies, are attending antique fairs and playing backgammon. Since the kids are naturally going to be attracted to things that are bad for them, it is regrettable that the standards of amorality are being set by creatures of such little grace and wit. Jim Morrison's sexual irregularities were probably no more troubling than those of a Tory Minister, but at least he looked terrific in leather trousers.

Bob Dylan was a bit of a fiend around the medicine cabinet, but his contribution to the global consciousness is far superior to that of a pill-popping jock trying to improve his personal best over 10,000 metres. Boyhood imaginations which were once fired up by tales of Bob Marley's incalculable progeny are now being fed sad slivers of erotica concerning the former Bishop of Galway.

Rock has handed over the keys of the kingdom of weirdness to a dreadful array of bores, blubberers and half-wits, creating a climate in which the uninteresting antics of a David Mellor can titillate a nation, and the Free World ponders the meaning of Bill Clinton's tiresome leaning towards oral sex. It is as though all the geeks of this world have been unleashed, while the relics of ould mayhem sit at home, counting their money.

Garth Brooks, President of the United States? It's about time they elected a good-living man.

The pale moon was rising. And it was a full moon, by all accounts.

Dr Mick Loftus warned us about this kind of thing. As he did before the World Cup, with similar futility, the former GAA major-domo spoke out against the culture of frenzied drinking which is synonymous with the Rose Of Tralee and other festivals of Gaeldom.

Plato was there before him. The great gay philosopher wanted to forbid wine to Under-18s, to offer it in moderation up to the age of 30, and to make it freely available only to people over 40. Hippocrates recorded the case of a man dying after over-indulging in sex and wine. "He complained of stiffness, vomiting, insomnia, palpitations, delirium and incoherent speech". And that was just the sex.

It is still pretty easy to find pillars of Kerry society who allege that the Rose Of Tralee festival thrives on its "family atmosphere". Why do they say things which they know to be absurd? Not much sign of the truth ever shining there. I have a friend from near Killorglin who doesn't go to the Rose any more, because at thirty, he thought that his constitution couldn't take all the drinking and rutting he would have to do in order to feel included. "It's like Feile for people with suits," he said. Except that at Feile, you can blame it on rock'n'roll and feckless youth, while The Rose is part of what we are.

Of course the analysis of Dr Mick Loftus, or Dr Dermot Clifford, or any other doctor since time immemorial, is spot on. Where a lot of people differ is that they regard the occasional festive atrocity as being good for the soul. This is why there was a crusade to free the man who mounted the Croppy Boy statue in Tralee, buck naked, and who got a year in jail, while the brother of the Texas Rose was fined a pittance for driving on the wrong side of the road and having no insurance cover. A large crowd had assembled to cheer him on as he sat astride the Croppy Boy, high on the improbability of it all. Was he not drawing an ironic parallel with the Puck Fair, where a goat stands naked for all to see, whether he likes it or not? In parts of New York City, they would call him a performance artist, and give him money.

And what of King Puck himself, the escort who saw his Rose home at midnight in mint condition, and who managed to have another woman in bed, making the beast-with-two-backs, by 2 a.m.? On the Jack Nicholson scale, this is pretty good going. In any man's language, this is fast work. The *bean an tí* thought different, and gave the girl her marching papers. No-one told her that it's a bit Irish in this day and age to be evicting women in the middle of the night, enacting the landlady's version of *coitus interruptus*.

"Have you a girl in there?" Six little words. So chilling.

The great and good of Tralee should be eternally grateful that the world's most ridiculous beauty contest was revitalised by authentic images of The Irish at Play.

By all accounts, the Irish are developing a taste for more exotic substances than mere porter. In an average lifetime, stumbling over two million quid while you are walking the dog will not be a recurring phenomenon. The odds are shortened, however, if you exercise your hound along the south and south-west coast of Ireland, where a mysterious magnetic force appears to draw large consignments of illegal drugs into its maw, washed ashore on the high tide.

Mr Patrick J MacNamara, a farmer and FAS supervisor, hit the jackpot when he discovered a package the size of two bales of briquettes on the shore near Fanore village in the Burren. It was heavily wrapped in plastic and netting, so Mr MacNamara clearly deduced that the package was not, in fact, two bales of briquettes. He reported it to the local Gardai, who quickly deduced that it was cocaine with a street value of £2 million.

There was some confusion here, because RTE reported the figure of £2 million, but the *Irish Times* priced it at around £3 million. I suppose it depends on how many movie moguls are in town for the weekend, but a million quid is a million quid, and quite a discrepancy, even if you are out of your gourd at the time of asking. Perhaps the *Times* is more *au fait* with current Dublin 4 prices than the Clousseaus of Clare.

Noting the incorruptible nature of the Irish people in general, the cocaine barons may wish to exploit this sense of probity by labelling their packages thus: "If undelivered, please return to P Escobar, P O Box 666, The Old Laboratory, The Jungle, Colombia, South America. Muchas gracias."

It is admittedly rare to find a bale of the Colombian marching powder lying on the beach, minding its own business. Usually it is cannabis resin which finds its way into the Bermuda Triangle adjacent to our shores, though the Garda response tends to be similar in the case of both. They issue a statement saying that there's a lot more where this lot came from, somewhere out at sea.

How do they know? Obviously, at any given time, there are a lot of drugs in transit on the high seas, but how do they know that this particular consignment is just a chip off the old block? They must be very clever. There is also a ritual whereby a detective is pictured holding up one of the packages, a faint flicker of melancholy in his eyes as he beholds the price of forty houses in Rathmines lying on the table in front of him. An entire block of Leinster Road, a multitude of bedsitters, neatly wrapped.

Invariably, the cannabis or cocaine is described as being "high-grade". How do they know, and what are they teaching them in Templemore these days? I await the day when our embattled Drugs Squad unveils its latest discovery as nothing much to write home about, a couple of kilos of ropey coke, tarted up with talcum powder and self-raising flour. I will await this day in vain, as long as the Gardai await the sort of funding they demand to fight them on the beaches.

They estimate that MacNamara's contraband was far too much for the Irish domestic market. How do they know? Are they aware of the number of international film projects coming this way?

You can't just feed them poitin, from our own laboratories. They are busy people.

They Don't March Against
Jazz No More

Ireland is a country in which there was once a march against Jazz. This glorious event happened in Leitrim, and it was inspired by a strong sense of cultural self-preservation. For the marchers, Jazz represented a threat to hallowed Gaelic standards, with its unabashed "jitterbugging" allied to the reputedly ungovernable appetites of the coloured peoples.

It was also their way of saying: "We are daft. We were born daft, all belonging to us are daft, and we will remain daft for as long as we can manage it, please God."

Things were simpler then, when the lines of demarcation between indigenous music and foreign muck were as clearly defined as the Cold War chasm between East and West. Even in the 70s, a leading dance-hall proprietor was able to place all music into three categories: Country'n'Western, Pop, and Mad Pop. Country'n'Western was self-explanatory, Pop would mean Gina, Dale Haze & The Champions, and Mad Pop was that rough beast slouching towards Babylon, carrying in its train a rabble of hairy hoors with heads full of hash, provoking the plain people to protest, "Sure, that's not music at all. It's just noise." Or, if you like, Thin Lizzy and Peggy's Leg.

Likewise, Establishment johnnies in Britain and America would agonise about 'dem jungle riddums which created frenzy where once there was peace, pandemonium where once there was order. It created a tension which was as necessary as the eternal conflict between youth and authority. If you weren't interesting enough to be regarded as some form of public menace, you were merely peddling cabaret.

Now that the culture formerly known as rock'n'roll can be seen to generate monstrous levels of revenue, those lines have been muddied beyond recognition. The Irish Government has now set up a Task Force, featuring committees which will report on marketing, technology, taxation, education, and a creative environment, with a view to generating more jobs on the music scene.

Jobs? Did somebody mention jobs?

As I understood it, if rock'n'roll was about anything, it was about avoiding all activity which could reasonably be described as a job. The Biz generated sundry activities such as hairdressing, fashion design, disc-jockeying, bouncing, roadie-ing, ligging, the manufacture and sale of drugs, the recruitment and distribution of groupies, record-plugging, chart-rigging, hotel demolition, and the wholesale exploitation of original artists, particularly black males from the Southern States by the name of Blind Lemon. But you wouldn't seriously regard any of that as work.

The Government's "taxation committee" contains representatives from IBEC and SFADCO, for Christ's sake. IBEC? SFADCO? Were ELP not bad enough? In the culture formerly known as rock'n'roll, the role of "committees" was to marshal the forces of darkness, preferably a colourful selection of full-blown balubas of the type which object to rock festivals on grounds of planning permission. They will always be with us, though there was a time when they represented the broad mainstream of public opinion, whereas now they are little fish swimming against the establishment tide. Those who marched against Jazz had it easy by comparison.

It seems a pity that the illusion of rock'n'roll as a counter culture, even as revolt-into-style, is no longer tenable, but there's no avoiding it. While it lasted, fatuous though it was, there was always the possibility of an outfit like The Sex Pistols emerging to make a few great records, while performing a useful social function.

Prince appeared a likely lad for a while, but he was last seen sporting a SLAVE tattoo in response to his contractual problems. Prince and George Michael, the last of the red hot rebels, railing

Declan Lynch

against the fine print of society, while Iggy Pop agonises over his golf handicap. Personally, I blame the disastrous Live Aid for starting the rot of universal bonhomie which has made the once feisty rock'n'roll circus such a repellant exercise in global accountancy. Patrick Kavanagh felt that there must be something inherently flawed in a work of his, if it was accessible to policemen. Similarly, the fact that no serious Irish politician will fail to salute "U2 and The Cranberries" is a sad day for a culture which spawned exotic beasts of the jungle such as Screamin' Jay Hawkins, P J Proby, and Motorhead. Those lads were well beyond the Pale of any Government Task Force, unless it was the type of Task Force charged with the solemn duty of exterminating them like dogs.

The committees for the advancement of rock'n'roll carry a distant echo of official drives to preserve Irish dancing, or flute-playing, or the ancient art of the melodeon-maker. A hard oul' station. Will we see the day when Ministers dispense with the formal *A Chara*, and greet constituents with "Awopbopalubop?" Will Ard-Fheiseanna drop *A Cairde Gael* in favour of "How're we doin' on the right side?" Will the corridors of Leinster House bear witness to deputies giving one another high-fives, saying "Free your ass and your mind will follow"?

Any day now...

172

It's Brooke Shields that you would really worry about. Should she ever go to a computer-dating agency, they will note the fact that close companions of hers include Liam Neeson and Michael Jackson. Any computer matching up the respective credentials of Liamo and Jacko would have to come up with a radically new species of being, the like of which has not been encountered before on this planet.

Speaking live to Oprah Winfrey at his ranch, Jacko declared his love for Brooke, though she reckoned that they are just good friends. Watching him speaking in that extraordinary timbre which suggests that he breakfasts on helium, you might think that with friends like that, you would get to enjoy your own company pretty soon.

The interview, his first in ten years, was perhaps the most obsequious exchange since Malcolm Muggeridge last sat down for an eyeball with Mother Theresa of Calcutta, albeit without the jokes and the streetwise banter. Psychologically speaking, Jacko was going through a heavy period of denial. Everything they say about him is false: all those stories about extensive plastic surgery, about him sleeping in an oxygen tent, about his unusually intimate relationship with the chimp, Bubbles, even about his reported insistence that Ms Winfrey introduce him as The King of Pop. The spectre of paedophilia had yet to raise its ugly head.

He owns up to a nose job, but in California, this is a basic cosmetic ritual on a par with one's morning ablutions. And on the subject of his alleged virginity, he does not discuss such matters, because, like St Patrick, he is a gentleman. One half-expected him to deny being the guy who sang 'Ben', about a rat with whom he was on friendly terms, or to refute allegations that he was once a member of the Jackson Five; and in a way, these would have a greater credibility than the other protestations.

To a large extent, he is not the person who used to sing with the Jackson Five, because, for a start, that person was Afro-American, and Oprah Winfrey's interviewee was plainly a white person. He says that there is something wrong with his skin pigmentation, causing the colour to drain from his cheeks, though I think that he just decided to reverse the old theatrical convention, by appearing in white-face. He has already confounded one ancient taboo by stating his preference for performing with children and animals, because they don't tell him lies. Nor, however, can they interpret all the facts at their disposal and tell him the truth.

Elizabeth Taylor apparently just happened to be wandering through the house, as you'd expect, and sat in for a few minutes to eulogise her fellow childhood star, who, despite what they say, is a thoroughly regular guy and an absolute barrel of laughs. The fact that, to this viewer, all parties to the proceedings were coming across as *bona fide* space cadets, added a piquant irony to this bizarre notion of Michael Jackson, the guy next door who just wants to break even. Admittedly, Liz Taylor was looking a lot better than Jacko, but then, Richard Burton is probably looking a bit better than Jacko these days.

Apart from those moments when he performed a few steps and sang a bar of a tune, there was little on display to alter the widely held perception that Jacko is as mad as a March hare. And I, for one, will defend to the death his inalienable right so to be. Of course the man is nuts. The idea of someone who has led the incredible life of Michael Jackson being anything else but nuts, is, in fact, nuts.

It is arguably part of the job of being Michael Jackson to have the most ridiculous speaking voice on Earth, to be the first person to successfully undergo a change of race, to have a teen-age crush on a rodent, or to want to marry Liz Taylor, as though she hadn't been through enough of that already. I have a remote suspicion that the man known to his brothers as "Smelly", because he was so good at sniffing out business deals, understands fully that this is all part of his vocation, and that the more he denies his eccentricity, the more bonkers he appears.

This might just be his way of staying ahead of the game. But I think that he is probably a genuine loon, which is fine, as long as he can afford it, and remains a danger only to himself.

STEVIE WONDER'S PENIS

Let me tell you about Stevie Wonder's penis. I'm telling you this for two reasons. First of all, it's a true story, and second of all, you'd go a long way to beat that as an opening line.

It goes something like this:

One day, a man by the name of Trubee, living and working — in a manner of speaking — on the west coast of America, saw an ad in a magazine. "We will put music to your words," it said. All you had to do was to send a few dollars to an address in Nashville, Tennessee, and you would receive a professional recording of your lyric. Christy Hennessy used to offer similar services when times were hard.

Trubee, who dabbled in the black arts of the music business such as disc-jockeying, composed what is arguably the most demented aggregation of words conceived by man, and called it 'Stevie Wonder's Penis'. Along with a meditation on the great man's appendage, it spoke of vile congress with visiting Martians, and substance abuse. The author despatched this document to Nashville, and duly received a swinging country'n'western interpretation of his work, with one alteration. They had changed the title to 'Blind Man's Penis'.

Otherwise, they let the lyrics stand as the author conceived them. To a mid-tempo country beat, a Nashville voice crooned the following: *"I got high last night on LSD/ My mind was beautiful, and I was free/ Warts love my nipples, because they are pink/ Vomit on me yeah, yeah, yeah./ A blind man's penis is erect because he's blind/ Is erect because he is blind/ Let's make love under the stars/ And watch for UFOs/ If little baby Martians come out of the UFO/ We'll fuck them, yeah, yeah, yeah."* And so it goes. This was released as a vinyl record, presumably on prescription only to registered addicts. I have seen it and heard it and it is out there.

One wonders what Stevie would have made of it all. I got an opportunity to ask him about it in Paris but declined the opportunity at the risk of creating an international incident. The scene was a press conference in the Meridian Hotel, where scores of European journalists had congregated to mark the release of *Conversation Peace*, Stevie's first major album since 1987. With the Belgians, the Swiss, the Norwegians, the Germans, and the French themselves asking all sorts of interesting and meaningful questions, I decided that it would be letting the side down somewhat for the Irish representative to throw 'Blind Man's Penis' into the ring. I upheld the dignity of my nation. I did it for all of us. And frankly, on the whole, it is better if Trubee's meisterwork remains a cult artefact, preferably sealed in a lead container and buried at the bottom of the sea.

Speaking of which, I asked Stevie about Newt Gingrich instead, and his plan to revive the orphanage concept: "Some people say he makes a lot of sense. I say he makes a lot of nonsense," the great man replied. It was the correct answer. Stevie also saluted the crumbling of the Berlin Wall, and the unification of Europe. He believes in the innocence of Michael Jackson, and thinks that Prince is a fine person. He found inspiration for the album in Ghana, which he regards as a kind of spiritual homeland. He reads the papers to keep abreast of global injustices, because watching CNN isn't enough.

Stevie Wonder has this slightly disconcerting habit of dropping in a line about watching television. He says that in the early days, as a boy phenomenon, when his minders were trying to get him to do interviews and the like, he would protest that he wanted to watch 'Huckleberry Hound' instead. He speaks of his blindness with much good humour, though the sleuths of Norway and Belgium were trying to get him onto a more solemn track. He firmly denied that he was spending a lot of money looking for a cure. He was in good form. But I still wasn't taking any chances on 'Blind Man's Penis'.

Stevie, all things considered, is a credit to the human race, and he deserves heavy respect. Motown founder Berry Gordy learned to respect him when Little Stevie turned twenty-one, and canceled all his contracts the day after Gordy had thrown a superb party to celebrate his coming of age. The lawyer who did the canceling was fired for his unmannerly timing, but a better one was hired to negotiate a mind-boggling $13 million deal, which included a clause forbidding Gordy to sell the label without Stevie's consent. You could let Stevie Wonder out.

At the Cite De La Musique, a wondrous modernist pleasure-dome opened in January 1995 by Francois Mitterand, Stevie performed tracks from *Conversation Peace*, seasoning the show with some of his immortal smash hits. Albert Reynolds would call it a super hall, though the pristine decor confirms that well-known Parisian disdain for flock wallpaper. Any fears that Stevie would provide the wallpaper proved groundless. It seems strange that Stevie would leave an eight-year gap between albums, because a voice of this quality could render recordings of the Yellow Pages, and do excellent business. It quickly obliterates the voices of the assembled Europeans, who have this infuriating knack of speaking English better than you do.

"I want to get to a better place every day," he says. He is only forty-four, though his career seems to have spanned a few millennia. There can't be many better places for him to get to, and with any luck at all, he will steer clear of Nashville. They do things differently there.

KEITH RICHARDS AND "THE LOGO OF CHRISTIANITY"

In the Summer of '95, the well-known rock group The Rolling Stones "kicked off" their European tour with a "gig" in Sheffield, England. It was their first British concert in five years, and it was completely sold out.

The self-styled Voodoo Lounge tour was expected to yield approximately £100 million in ticket sales alone, though much greater revenue would accrue from the sale of souvenirs and gimcracks. In addition to playing a selection of their popular "hits" such as the famous 'Satisfaction', 'Jumping Jack Flash', and 'Brown Sugar', the group would be expected to sell some cars from the Volkswagon range.

In a £6 million sponsorship deal, the German auto giant created "the fabulous new Volkswagon Golf Rolling Stones collection", a limited edition available in standard saloon format, or in what experts describe as an ultra-sporty two-door convertible cabriolet, with alloy wheels, CD-player, a white gear-stick with the Rolling Stones logo, and the group's name stitched into the seat fabric.

By the end of the tour, the corporation (Volkswagon not the Stones) expected to sell 150,000 of these ultra-sporty wagons at £6,000 a pop. Book now to avoid disappointment. A VW spokesperson remarked: "We want to be associated with something as lively as the Rolling Stones." Lively, eh? It's a peculiar word, lively, to describe these emperors of rock'n'roll. But then it is also remarkably appropriate to write about their current activities in the style of the annual report of a merchant bank. "Lively" is a word that is normally associated with successful tea-dances or Sales of Work, where the participants are under some form of medication.

I suppose the Strolling Bones are also at that stage of life when they acquire their drugs by prescription only. It was not always thus. While no Stone would be seen dead in a Volkswagon, their career can be likened to that of the legendary Beetle, and I don't mean John Lennon. The ancient engine still splutters into action for a spin around the block, if you ask it nicely. The body work may be frayed around the edges, but with a new spray of paint and a bit of panel-beating, you could hardly tell the difference. It needs a good rest after every journey, and frequent oil-changes, a bit like Keith Richards when he used to go to Switzerland to have his blood changed after polluting himself.

Hitler had a great gra for the old Volkswagon. He emerged from the bierkellers to play the big stadiums too, but his act came to a chundering halt, while the Stones go on forever, rolling over new territories. And fans of the Stones are as sentimental about the old brutes as the most loyal Beetle-owners, rejecting all the latest models in favour of the old reliable. It will take a lot more than two grand to get that heap of scrap off the roads.

Other than nostalgia, corporate entertainment, and pure greed, is there a respectable reason for the Stones to be prancing around in this unseemly fashion?

I feel that there is. It is a shockingly complicated way of going about it, but another Strolling Bones outing is the best way of keeping Keith Richards amused. And Keith Richards should be kept amused, now that he can enjoy a Stones concert in a state of full consciousness, or something approaching it. For many years, he was hearing about these mighty Rolling Stones concerts all over the world, and often, he must have thought, "I wish I was there." He was there, in a manner of speaking, cranking out those dirty old riffs and falling about the place, but his mind was on a different planet. It was an out-of-body experience which lasted for a very long time, and which deprived him of a lot of the simple pleasures of life, like a good night out at a Stones gig. It is important to always bear in mind that this man once described the Crucifix as the "logo" of Christianity. It is important to keep him amused, because he can say some silly things in idle moments, like when he discouraged young people from taking drugs. The American comedian Denis Leary pointed out the fatuity of this. There are no drugs left in the world, because Keith, the fucker, has taken the lot.

He endured some of the ennui described by the existential philosophers as they mourned the inability to truly seize the moment, or to appreciate an experience with intensity. "Why am I here? What am I doing here? What are all these people doing here anyway?" The eternal questions. Reflecting on his former lifestyle, he must occasionally get the feeling that when he straps on his trusty axe and lurches to the front of the stage with a fag hanging out of his gob, he is the first legend of rock to perform posthumously.

What you are actually seeing is little short of a resurrection, a miracle, an apparition made flesh, or whatever it is that encases his indestructible old bones. Unlike the fabled apparitions of Medjugorje, this one plays the guitar and sings, and poses for photographers, and is occasionally available for interview, drinking copiously from a bottle of Jack Daniels. For a man who once described the epitome of embarrassment as "turning blue in someone else's bathroom", there is no shame.

MACCARTHYISM

It must be strange being Jimmy MacCarthy, but then, as they might say on 'Thought For the Day', it must be strange being anyone.

The particular strangeness in the life of Jimmy MacCarthy is the near-impossibility of walking more than fifty yards without hearing one of his songs being rendered in any number of ways, not all of them pleasing to the ear.

There are times when he must get the eerie impression that he is being followed. By himself. Or by people impersonating him. From out of a record-shop, he is almost certain to hear a Christy Moore or a Mary Black or even a Phil Coulter number written by him. He will be reminded again that Christy's reading of 'Ride On' has a subtle twist of emphasis on the words "see you". This is important to him.

Mary Black might have shaved off the odd verse, and he will wonder why. With Phil Coulter, he may chuckle to himself and ponder the many ways in which he can spend the money. Perhaps he will give some of it away to one of the buskers who are interrupting his reverie by tearing 'Bright Blue Rose' limb from limb in his presence. Yes, he might pay them to go away. "Here, have a drink on Phil Coulter."

And one for himself? No, not really.

Jimmy doesn't go to pubs much any more, having retired from active drinking and smoking and carousing some years ago, but also, I suspect, due to the inevitability of hearing an inebriated minstrel singing 'As I Leave Behind Neidin' in a way that nature did not intend. That would put you off pubs, and people too. Like Yeats, it would make you wonder if your words had sent certain men out to do terrible things.

Here, I must confess a slight interest. 'Neidin' is partly written by me. I ran into Jimmy in Cork's Pizzaland shortly after its unveiling, and noted that he was pronouncing the word "rhododendron" as "rhododendrom". "Get rid of the *m*, James, and your pension is secure," I said. And so it came to pass. For its inclusion on one of his instrumental all-time classics, I think it is fair to say that Phil Coulter owes me about 17p.

Surrounded on all sides by imitations of himself, seeing distorted images of Jimmy Mac in a hall of cracked mirrors, he decided some three years ago that the essence of MacCarthyism could only be found within himself. The album *Song Of The Singing Horseman* was the first full-blown version of His Master's Voice, laying down the blueprints for others to follow, getting his retaliation in first. Then he produced *The Dreamer*, a collection which establishes him further as a first-rate interpreter of Jimmy MacCarthy songs. Perhaps the finest in Europe.

It is as if a top designer (like models, designers are always "top") took to modelling his own clothes. This is the way to go. It is somewhat different to Brendan Behan interrupting his own plays to show the actors how to do it properly. However much you might enjoy such Rabelaisian interventions, you could not say that here was a man in control.

But MacCarthyism still has a collaborative dimension. He toured the country with a rainbow coalition of himself, Mick Hanly, Don Baker, and Finbarr Furey, called 'Four For The Road'. It could be viewed as a riposte to the "Woman's Heart" experience, something on the lines of "A Man's By-Pass". Each of them could be relied upon to bring his own constituency activists to the party, and perhaps to object from the floor to statements made by the coalition partners.

Jimmy jokes that his people never showed up. Or were keeping pretty quiet about it if they did. In fact he transcends all parties and pressure groups. Finbarr Furey's people are also his people, whether they know it or not. Finbarr has sung MacCarthy too. It was getting lonely out there on the lake.

One night on television, I saw some scenes of Cork which featured a busker singing 'The Mad Lady And Me', the thinking man's version of 'The Banks', a true story in which a woman actually jumps into the Lee, threatening to swim out to sea. It was written by...eh...Jimmy MacCarthy, the first of his songs that I had heard all day.

Like the woman in the river, Jimmy had his own way of doing things eventually.

There is a distinct feeling of science fiction about all this, from the moment you paste that Day Pass to your lapel, and enter the land of Eurovision. It is a strange land, a surreal place, situated on a different planet to the one which we earthlings call "home". As you approach the Point of no return, you are aware of a friendly but intensive security presence, a lot of walkie talkies and mobile phones and "Can I help you, Sir?" There is a scanner which detects whatever metal objects you may wish to hurl.

You have to keep reminding yourself that this is, after all, the Eurovision Song Contest, and not a summit meeting of world leaders. Will there be strip-searching too, or is that just on request? You resist the temptation to sign yourself in as Carlos the Jackal, Music Lover. It's a bit early in the day for a diplomatic incident.

I was drawn into this parallel universe by the 'Pat Kenny Show', on which I was a guest, talking about Eurovision. I had a reason to be there, and I could leave whenever I liked. Just passing through. Yet, there is a kind of mesmeric fascination to this ethereal land which draws you into its maw, a sense that you are in a different time-zone, where normal states of being no longer apply.

A lot of people, for example, are here just because they're here. They are milling and mingling, just Being There. They have been beamed down to the Point for reasons which are mysterious and obscure. They are at the Point, and somehow Pointless. Here, they can take photographs of RTE people, or get an authentic Eddie Friel autograph. Wednesday is RTE day, and the place is inundated with RTE operatives, evacuated for the day to that spot down by the river, to lay the blanket on the ground. There's Pat, and Ronan, and Larry, and there's the 2FM Roadcaster, ye gods. Wonderful things.

There's Paddy Power the bookmaker, or his representative on Earth, explaining to callow Europeans how to place a bet. Putting my tank on Norway at 10/1, I note that you can also bet on John Major leading the Conservatives into the next election, on Arsenal winning the Cup-Winners Cup, and United for the Premiership. Reminders of a distant civilisation.

Gingerly, almost fearfully, like Harold Carter gazing for the first time at the tomb of Tutankhamen, I cross the portals of the theatre, where the Spanish entry is rehearsing. When they have done their Iberian thing, a wild burst of applause erupts from a section of the crowd. These must be the Spanish "delegates", and believe me, they are giving it a bit of welly. You would think that they were home and dry already, that Spain had cracked it, and that it was time to loosen their expense accounts at the bar, a hail of *pesetas* flying over the counter like so much confetti.

Ah yes, the bar. You need one of them.

There is a sign in the bar which reads: "Mobile Free Zone. No Thank You. Non merci. No Gracias. Nein Danke. Ne Tak. Possession of a mobile phone punishable by £500 fine. If you persist, we will confiscate your Campari and your Gucci watch." The wit of the Irish.

At this stage, I am presenting an unusual face to the world. The bar has run out of cigarettes, so I opt for a cigar instead. For the career smoker, the absence of ciggies induces a sort of panic, a defiant feeling that you would smoke the Finnish entry if you had to. Unfortunately, a rake of people who are known to me arrive along, see me chomping on a cigar at the bar, and think that I have gone a bit peculiar. Only at Eurovision.

A Belgian couple are handing around photographs, trophies of Eurovisions past. These people arrange their holidays to coincide with Eurovision. They see it as a last bastion of "live music", so they do. You know that such people must exist, but they still make you nervous. The real world that you have left behind now seems so far away. You hope that it will still be there when all this is over.

Now you are becoming too familiar with the ambiance, beginning to distinguish the inhabitants of planet Eurovision by their demeanour, laminates unseen. To paraphrase Wodehouse, the journalists are laughing like hyenas who have just heard a good one from another hyena; the "delegates" are trying to look ambassadorial, pleased to meet their counterparts, straining at the leash of protocol; the musicians have a strange, haunted look about them, pensive and sombre, wondering if they should have turned back at that fork in the road. For them, it seemed to be more of a hum than a buzz, that unearthly sound emerging from the belly of the beast. Their sleep would be infested with unquiet dreams.

So Norway won, at least on paper. In reality, it was another Irish triumph, with Fionnuala Sherry doing the business on what sounded like an eccentric Clannad B-side. That's why I backed it, and why I told anyone who would care to listen that it was going to win pulling up. Ireland's name was on the trophy once more, and thanks to Paddy Power's generous odds, I sometimes think that I made more out of Eurovision than Charlie McGettigan and Paul Harrington combined. Remember, the talented Paul had to give that jacket back to RTE at the end of the year. I will still have my jacket when it all begins again in Oslo.

Who can fathom the genius of a nation? The Italians have the best cars, the best football, the best ancient ruins, the best traffic-jams, and the best organised crime. We have no peers at literature, porter-brewing, emigration, coursing, and Eurovision.

The gods bestow their gifts in uneven ways, and we have graciously accepted the crown of Eurovision kings, pledged to treat it as an honourable estate, where others, for excellent reasons of their own, would be mortified. How can we nourish this terrible genius, and lead the nations of Eurovision caterwauling like poisoned pups into the next millennium? How can we make Ireland and Eurovision totally synonymous, as Greece is with bottom-pinching?

The rock writer Bill Graham has proposed a Eurovision Summer School to shame those cerebral hooleys which celebrate windbags like Yeats and Shaw. With masterclasses by Shay Healy and Johnny Logan, ceremonial readings from old issues of "Spotlight", and a folk-mass with Dana to round off the proceedings in suitably revivalist style, this Summer School would attract tons of foreign currency, and possibly even teach the Eurovision formula to some other bugger who can take it off our hands for a while.

We must also make it a permanent feature of the tourist's itinerary by banging something down in bricks and mortar and asphalt. I suggest the Boulevard d'Eurovision, featuring the paw-prints of all our Euro entrants since 1965, Year Zero. Butch Moore, Sean Dunphy, Cathal Dunne, Red Hurley, Sheeba, the lot. You would also have the cloven hoof-prints of all those who lost out in the National Song Contest, as a reminder of the barbarism which we strove to overcome, armed only with a penchant for cod-American ballads. Johnny Logan, of course, must have a whole boulevard to himself. And we already have a Harrington Street.

The universities must respond with new Eurovision departments, offering courses in the technical, philosophical and ethical dimensions, as well as practical demonstrations from visiting Professors of Schlock, passing through on their way to Clontarf Castle. Graduates will be awarded a Bachelor of Studies in Eurovision degree, or BSE, which, coincidentally, is also the acronym for mad cow disease. The Government can finesse the dole queues by organising FAS courses in Euro-craft, with Brendan Graham as national co-ordinator. The only difference between this and other FAS courses is that you'll have a better chance of winning the Eurovision than of getting a job.

Staging the Eurovision will pose greater challenges to our Gaelic ingenuity with each passing year. Every bucklepper from

Buncrana to Buttevant is looking for the Grand Prix to be held in his town, in his street, nay, in his house. But we must leave this to our gnarled army of professionals. Will they opt for kinder, gentler Eurovisions, or will they crank up the levels of excess until they are left with no alternative but to stage live human sacrifices at half-time? As the credits roll at the end, will we see "Director: Caligula!"?

But then, like most of the things that make us happy, Eurovision can be bad for your health. As we sweated bullets for Gerry Ryan, collapsing with relief when Cynthia Ni Mhurchu remembered the capital of Finland, my partner turned to me and said, "Isn't it terrible, all the same, to be frightened in your own home?"

"No-one remembers who won the Eurovision Song Contest last year," said Pierce Brosnan at a gala performance on VE Day in London. Bollocks, Pierce. It was Paul Harrington and Charlie McGettigan singing 'Rock'n'Roll Kids', written by Brendan Graham. Everyone knows that.

He went on to say that everyone remembers *Riverdance*, now trading as *Riverdance — The Show*, and the biggest thing since sliced bread.

Riverdance — The Show was predictably awful. A tacky round-up of jaded hoofers from around the world, it was too portentous and pompous to be even regarded as acceptable kitsch. This was the confirmed vulgarian's idea of high culture, so it was hardly surprising that the opening night was attended by a shatteringly philistine herd of politicians and dinner-jacketed nonentities, who could look at one another across the banqueting hall and see a constellation of megastars. A posse of barely literate hacks wrestled with the language in vain, and, thoroughly defeated, were scarcely surprised to find that they had all written the same thing: "Irish dancing is sexy." It was another wretched night for Ireland.

Careful with that axe, ma'am, I haven't actually seen *Riverdance — The Show*. But if I had seen it, and had penned something along the lines of the above, it is certain that I would be regarded as not just mad, but a traitor too. Not just bonkers, but a begrudger, the begrudger's begrudger, the begrudger that professional begrudgers call "The Guvnor".

We can't get enough of a good thing in this country. There is an addictive strain in the psyche which compels us to go completely doo-lally en masse whenever something exciting is done in our name. Thus, a Riverdance agnostic would not only be regarded as extremely weird, he would be suspected of what Charlie Haughey used to call "national sabotage". I think the colloquial term is "tearing the hole out of it". Tearing the hole out of it is often an immensely enjoyable experience, but it can go horribly wrong.

Leaving Riverdance in dry dock as a phenomenon are the adventures of the Irish football team. When Spain ran in three goals against us at Lansdowne Road, as though we were a pub eleven up in the Phoenix Park, it was something more than a thrashing. It seemed to verge on the criminal, like swarthy Johnny Spaniard barging into a kiddies' birthday party and splattering the cake all over the walls. Phenomena die hard. When Jack's lads were hauled back to the Phoenix Park after a good thrashing in America, the embarrassment was palpable. We had finally had too much of a good thing.

Michael Carruth wins our first Olympic gold medal since the Bronze Age, and Biblical scenes of rejoicing ensue, while the Cuban fighters slope away, not entirely happy with the mere seven golds that they picked up that morning. Stephen Roche wins the Tour De France, and the Taoiseach materialises on the podium. He is a god. And Stephen is immortal too, arriving home to scenes which make a Cecil B De Mille production look like excerpts from Beckett. Great men all, they seem pleasantly bewildered to have become phenomena, to hear politicians extolling their achievements, and using their names in tortuous analogies. Like U2, Zig and Zag, and even Roddy Doyle, they are now liable to be mentioned in garbled despatches from Leinster House.

In America and Europe, Garth Brooks is a big country star. In Ireland, he is a phenomenon. The howdy-hats are out too for line-dancing, that galloping virus which seems set to claim the majority of the adult population. It is all fun and games, and harmless lunacy, and a bit of oul' sport. But I ask this question: How the hell did we give ourselves the reputation of being a nation of begrudgers?

We take to things with the almost hysterical abandon of children on Christmas morning. Perhaps begrudgery is just an absence of frenzy, and the begrudgers are the ones who have to give us all a ride home.

THE DICEMAN

Those who were part of Dublin in the rare oul' times speak a lot about street characters such as Johnny Fortycoats and Bang Bang. Some would say that they speak of little else.

It seems to suggest that in the rare oul' times, the poor were more picturesque, and that Mr Fortycoats and Mr Bang somehow rose above the squalor to make something of their lives, and to give everyone a good laugh while they were at it. A bit like Eamon MacThomais meets the Progressive Democrats. Through this window of nostalgia, one sees these characters as improvisers around a single theme. I gather that Johnny Fortycoats wore many coats, while Bang Bang used to go up to people in the street, assume the position, and say, "Bang Bang, you're dead. " Those were the days.

Street theatre was in its infancy at the time, and these men were essentially free spirits who fused their lives with their art in a random fashion. They are fondly remembered by many people who never actually saw them. Such is the nature of street legends in the rare oul' times.

Tom McGinty, The Diceman, had become such a legend, that RTE radio's 'This Week' programme interviewed him on his retirement. 'This Week's' departure from its sombre, state-of-the-nation style suggested that a significant personage had left the national stage. It was the sort of thing they do when a political veteran cashes in his chips, reminiscing about his meetings with great men, and the support he has received from one good woman.

Unlike Fortycoats and Bang Bang, The Diceman had a flexible repertoire. In common with them he had poverty, and a bit of hassle from the Gardai. His performances developed out of an urge to discover interesting ways of begging. Arriving from Scotland to find a dearth of opportunity for a man of his talents, he noted that half the country seemed to be begging in one form

192

or another, so he worked up an act which involved winking at his benefactors as a quid pro quo, or a quid pro quid.

He became the King of the Beggars, a Daniel O'Connell for the 1980s, each appearance in Grafton Street a sort of informal Monster Meeting addressed by a mute orator. This may serve to explain the enormous outpouring of affection on his retirement, including a gala evening at the Olympia Theatre in his honour, with hundreds of people on the pavement outside, hoping for a few ticket cancellations.

Being There was important to them, because The Diceman literally stood for something. He was the one fixed point in an expanding Universe, until he moved. You couldn't really call it mime, because it was too funny for that. Watching a man pretending to milk an invisible cow may strike you as being pretty clever, but it does not elicit guffaws from passing pedestrians. When it becomes particularly pretentious, you can feel like tapping Sergeant Furriskey on the shoulder, and suggesting that he move the mime artiste to another location. France, for example.

Nor was it Performance Art, for which we were truly grateful. The Diceman had a touch of anarchy, a sense that he shouldn't really be doing this, but that the good burghers would decide. His Dracula was a masterpiece, his sackcloth-and-ashes was a hoot, but I particularly enjoyed his Tina Turner, presenting a huge cheque to SPUC on the steps of their headquarters, for legal fees screwed out of the students. Here was a moving statue which did not tell you to repent, for the end is nigh, urge you to say The Rosary, or ask you to pray for the restoration of chastity. The Diceman took the moving statue out of the grotto and onto the streets, making it an ecumenical phenomenon, a thing steeped in democracy.

It was a savage irony that Tom McGinty's first intimations of illness involved a loss of balance, appearing to be drunk without having had the benefit of a night on the beer. This was Beethoven going deaf, the most well-balanced man in the country unable to stop himself from staggering.

There was a grandeur about his retirement from public life, marked by his appearance in the "royal box" of The Olympia, accepting the love and respect of a grateful nation.

He moved through the fair.

CHRISTY MOORE HAS NEVER HAD A DRINK WITH A MODEL

Christy Moore has been gelded and he doesn't like it. He takes a certain proprietary interest in the horse of that name who was snipped after some uninspiring performances. "Mind you, coming last at the Curragh is nothing new to me," he reflects. "I mitched there and I swam there," says the former boy soprano as he recalls adolescent renditions of "Have you ever been in love, me boys, and have you felt the pain?"

Having horses named after you, being billed in Germany as a "legendary folk idol", and looking forward to packing out the Point Theatre and the Cork Opera House for six consecutive nights can induce a sense of inner peace in a body. Christy's ten-night residency at The Point was a new breakthrough for a man whose idea of stage pyrotechnics is to press his vest before the show: "I would play places like the Concert Hall and wonder was I losing the run of myself? Shouldn't I be in the Baggot Inn instead? But the people were glad that I was there, so who was I to argue?"

His carefully honed schedule has allowed him the opportunity to fully indulge what amounts to an almost unnatural interest in the minutiae of Gaelic football in Kildare. He might attend three matches on the one day in the company of people who are "very famous in Newbridge". He favours the Lilywhites over Lillie's Bordello, though he is curious about the goings-on in said Bordello, stomping ground of many fellow celebrities. He asks the extraordinary question: "Would you be encouraged to bring your guitar and sing a few songs?"

Christy further mulls over the fact that in all his days, he has never had a drink with a model, and that it's probably too late now. This, and the notion that he must be the last remaining person in Ireland who has never met Ronnie Wood. No, when Christy is out among his people, they just laugh at him: "I love when I go into a place and people burst out laughing," he says. "It's a kind of shyness on their part, I suppose. Or at least I hope it is. And I like stopping at a petrol station and being asked, 'Have I got the right man?' How do you answer that?"

Though no longer the life and soul of the Artists' Bar, he perceives a kind of orgiastic continuity between the *Fleadh Ceoils* of old and events like *Feile*, where he entertained 50,000 people in a Tipperary Monsoon: "Back then, we were basically trying to do the same thing — to have a good time and get our end away. Maybe hear a new song. I was always chasing songs, others were chasing different things." He was flabbergasted, though, at the backstage facilities at *Feile* by comparison with more bucolic times: "I had two dressing rooms. One for changing in, for wringing out the vest, and another with bowls of fruit, and buffet facilities, and my own personal security guard. It was like Ascot, and a very far cry from Lisdoonvarna."

He reminisces about those endless barmy days of conspicuous consumption, when a legendary folk idol was expected to have a legendary thirst and capacity for liquor..."A nice snug in the afternoon...another gin'n'tonic...you just signal to the barman and he knows...light up another Major...lovely." These days, Christy pursues the less precarious Nirvana of the healthy mind in the healthy body, with a daily Zen-like constitutional around the environs of Dun Laoghaire pier. He looks twenty years younger than he did twenty years ago: "I did it all, and I really enjoyed it for most of the time I was doing it," he says. "But I don't miss it at all. It's an energy and an age thing. If your body's in a certain nick, and your head is in a certain nick, it's fine. But there's no crack in it any more when you're just a sot. You tend to get isolated. That's the time to get the fuck out of it."

He ponders his social diary with relish — Ireland v Denmark on the box, a rugby match on Saturday, a new episode of 'Taggart', the mandatory bit of slashing at a Gaelic games venue on Sunday, and Glenroe. Mainly he will prepare for the scarifying prospect of standing in front of the multitudes at The

Point and the Opera House, adorned only with an acoustic guitar and approximately five chords, and an unerring mainline into the better instincts of the nation.

The audience will do anything for him other than buy his T-shirts, thousands of which were run up to promote the album, *Smoke And Strong Whiskey*.

"There is a Christy Moore T-shirt mountain out there somewhere," he says. Is it not fragrant?

RORY GALLAGHER, 1948-1995

There is a tribe of us out there who woke up on a Thursday morning with a bad case of the blues. Rory had passed on the previous night, and his records were all over the radio. We mourned a lost leader.

For this tribe of thirtysomethings, the Gallagher gigs at the National Stadium were easily the most important cultural, and indeed religious experiences, of our teen-age years. On that Thursday morning, I doubt if there was a single member of the tribe who was not transported back to those nights of magic, remembering the good of it all. At a time when the musical life of the nation was dominated by dubious show bands and light entertainers, the Horslips kept us going during the year, and then the Messiah himself would duck-walk among us at Christmas. Rory, Rory, Rory. He was christened Liam, in Ballyshannon, but he preferred Rory, because as far as he knew, there was no Saint Rory. Not yet, anyway.

Bus-loads of pilgrims in their lumberjack shirts would arrive from all over the country to worship the great man. One of our own, too. One of our own. For me, and many others, Rory at the Stadium was a rite of passage. You would never feel quite the same about anything again. You had seen the promised land, and you liked it.

For some reason, in my flashback on that Thursday morning, I particularly remembered his demon bass-player, Gerry McEvoy, who spent most of the night rooted to the one spot, legs spread wide apart. The joke went that Gerry was a cardboard cut-out who was wheeled into the same position every night by the crew. But that rumbling in the foundations of the Stadium was real enough.

Gerry was one cool operator, all right, but we loved Rory like a brother. Up North, they were crazy about him, because in the darkest dog-days of the Troubles, when every other entertainer would sooner play Russian Roulette than play Belfast, Rory never missed a gig. Mind you, at that time, very few international superstars, or international anythings, played Dublin either. It is impossible to overstate the importance of Rory Gallagher, or the scale of his achievements.

There was many a show-band musician who tinkered away with a blast of Hendrix in the back of the wagon, but who put away such childish things to don the show-band fatigues, and churn out the old reliables for the unfortunate punters. Rory, and only Rory, exploded out of that melancholy world to form Taste, and through a combination of incredible talent, uncompromising integrity, and rootsy charisma, became a bloody star all over Europe. He was a comet in a land of glow-worms. Rock stars are now general all over Ireland, but Rory was the first. There was nothing remotely like him. He was not so much the Columbus of Irish rock as its Brendan The Navigator.

The tribe mourns him, and their own lost innocence at those National Stadium exorcisms, but for Rory, the road went on for ever. "I've toured more than any other artist in Europe," he told Liam Fay in *Hot Press*. "I've toured too much for my own good. It hasn't left time for very much else, unfortunately. You don't develop any family life or anything like that, and it makes all your relationships very difficult. There's always a certain percentage missing from your life. As a human being, you only have so much to give."

He would say that "the Blues are bad for your health. It's as simple as that. Jimmy Reid was epileptic. Howlin' Wolf ended up on a kidney machine. Most of the other big names were alcoholics. Muddy Waters was one of the few guys who got it under control."

Muddy Waters was probably his supreme hero, and until his own severe liver problems took hold, damage which doctors attributed to "accidental overdoses of medication", Rory fancied that he would emulate Muddy, still on top of the case in his sixties, getting stronger as he went along. Rory checked out at forty-seven.

My brief encounters with the man revealed a very shy person, and a transparently decent human being. He was sentimental about, and voraciously interested in Ireland, and whether in London, Paris, or Munich, he would try to pick up RTE radio most nights. He recalled getting a buzz out of picking up an Election Night broadcast in Paris, listening to John Bowman counting them in and counting them out. The Irish Sunday papers were a must, and he had a consuming interest in musical developments back home. "I'm constantly thinking about Ireland," he said. "I'd really like to go back there, eventually."

Rory almost joined the Rolling Stones, once, but was spared that pantomime by the skin of his teeth.

The story goes that after an incendiary performance at the Shrine Auditorium in LA, he instructed his brother and manager, Donal, to bar access to the dressing-room while he recovered. Donal turned away a chap with straggly hair and a scarf, but managed to retrieve him later on. It was Bob Dylan, coming to pay his respects to one of the greats.